Recognition for translation of a Latin American classic

"In 1937, three years after the publication of Insularismo, Antonio Pedreira's book on Puerto Rican identity, members of the police force in the city of Ponce opened fire on a crowd of nationalist demonstrators led by a contingent of young cadets and women in nurses' uniforms. I mention 'The Ponce Massacre,' as it came to be known, because the bloody incident became emblematic of the passions surrounding the question of national sovereignty in Puerto Rico. Today Pedreira's scholarly, rather aloof take on the question of national identity is undoubtedly a canonical text, which means that it is a prestigious, if rather musty, cultural artifact from a bygone era. Yet in rereading *Insularismo* today, something of the passion of those years of struggle for a measure of autonomy and self-determination should be kept in mind.

Pedreira's essay has roots in a powerful tradition that affirms the cultural and even the spiritual autonomy of 'Our America,' to borrow the title of José Martí's famous essay, in the face of the encroaching might of the United States. Today readers may find that some of the ideas presented in *Insularismo* are at best anachronistic, at worst downright offensive. For example, Pedreira repeats the well-worn notion that climate is destiny, and that the tropics undermine creative energies and make folks passive and childlike, that is, easy prey for the colonizer: hence the call-to-arms to overcome such limitations and everything associated with them.

One should bear in mind that *Insularismo* ignited polemic and controversy from the day it was published. Tomás Blanco, another great essayist from Pedreira's own 'Generation of 1930,' argued powerfully against Pedreira, notably in *El prejuicio racial en Puerto Rico* (Racial Prejudice in Puerto Rico), which was presented as a lecture in San Juan in 1937, the year of the infamous massacre in Ponce, and published five years later. Polemical and often polarizing in their arguments, both texts aided in the construction of an influential, however flawed, narrative of national unity in the face of a fragmented reality. If in the 1930s such fragmentation threatened the very existence of Puerto Rico's 'great family,' as a powerful national myth, subsequent generations of scholars and artists have explored the ways that fragmentation has led not just to violence and chaos but also to areas of rich and rewarding cultural productions.

I am honored to have played a small part in Aoife Rivera Serrano's translation of *Insularismo*; the earliest drafts of her work were undertaken in a translation class that I taught at The Graduate Center of the City University of New York. As a translator, Rivera Serrano was fascinated by the rhetorical flourishes of *Insularismo* and the challenges they presented. As a Puerto Rican living in New York, she recognized the obvious flaws in Pedreira's dated theses, yet felt personally touched by the polemic they ignited. Her translation has been a labor of love, making a major Puerto Rican work never before published in English accessible in that language. I believe that her work comes from a desire to give something back and to forge, as so many others have done, her own link with her island nation. Rivera Serrano's *Insularismo* is an important contribution to what should be an ongoing debate, not just on Puerto Rican politics and culture but also on the culture and politics of our hemisphere."

> —**Oscar Montero,** professor, Lehman College and
> The Graduate Center of the City University
> of New York, author of *José Martí: An Introduction*.
> (Palgrave Macmillan, 2004).

"Despite Puerto Rico's having been bound by long-standing and deep political and historical ties to the United States for more than 100 years, ask most English-speaking people about the status and history of Puerto Rico, and their answers will be vague at best, factually incorrect at worst. There are many reasons for this, chief among them Puerto Rico's ambiguous status as a 'commonwealth' of the United States; but another reason is language. Most of Puerto Rico's enormously important, rich and varied intellectual history has never been translated into English. This state of affairs results in a kind of absence in the United States' cultural imagination of the island, one that has worked to erase any sense of a sophisticated Puerto Rican contribution to the Americas—including, of course, to the United States itself. This is a particularly poignant fact for the generations of Puerto Ricans and other Latinos raised in the United States whose Spanish may only be partial, or even nonexistent. Translations of work from the early part of the century, when the educated elite of Puerto Rico began to argue issues still debated today, are especially necessary in order to negotiate, as Aoife Rivera Serrano notes, their sometimes 'rococo' Spanish.

As scholars and readers of Puerto Rican intellectual thought know, Antonio S. Pedreira stands as the best-known and possibly most important intellectual of the 'Generation of 1930.' He wrote and taught during a period in Puerto Rican letters when the question of a distinctly Puerto Rican character—or soul, as Pedreira himself put it—was hotly debated. Pedreira's answer to this question, his 1934 text titled *Insularismo*, was a document that reflected his own class position as well as many of the most important European and Latin American philosophical assumptions of the day, particularly as they concerned the modernizing influences of the *gigante al Norte*, the United States. Many of the assumptions and conclusions in Pedreira's text—the 'insularism' of Puerto Ricans, the 'docility' of their character, even the racialist assumptions about the 'inferiority' of the island's African heritage —have survived and sometimes even thrived in discussions of the Puerto Rican 'character' both on and off the island. For this reason alone Pedreira's text should be available in both Spanish and English; as Puerto Rican critic Juan Flores notes, these texts must be studied anew in order to understand the source, as well as the force, of such assumptions.[1] But another reason pertains here: *Insularismo* also stands as one of the first and most important moments of affirmation of a distinctly Puerto Rican sensibility—if not a national sense of itself, at least a cultural sense of itself—in contradistinction to the United States' discourse of Puerto Ricans as a weak and inferior people.

Aoife Rivera Serrano's translation of *Insularismo* is a necessary step in a kind of 'recovery' of Puerto Rican letters for those

[1] "The value of *Insularismo* in developing a critique [of ideas of Puerto Rican "character"] is its pivotal position within an extended controversy..."(19). Juan Flores, *Divided Borders: Essays on Puerto Rican Identity* (Arte Público Press, 1993).

Reviews

living on the mainland. Citing Pedreira's own maxim that 'language is the vault in which the embodiment of a people is deposited,' the translator is careful to keep the 'rococo' strangeness of Pedreira's rhetorical style while using a language that is clear to contemporary readers. Indeed, this translation captures nicely Pedreira's own sense of irony and even his sense of humor. Blasting the Puerto Rican taste for flowery rhetoric, for example, Pedreira traces 'our rhetoricalness' to the fact that as a colonized society, writers and thinkers used their 'archaic' Peninsular-oriented education 'in protective, superfluous verbosity.' Finishing his point with a wonderfully clear image, Pedreira maintains that cheap patriotic verbiage must be removed with a metaphor-ical 'well-aimed, collective blow to the mouth' so as to 'remove the homeland from our lips so that we, then, might be able to give it asylum in our hearts.' This sense of language, of irony and of Pedreira's deep commitment to Puerto Rico is captured in Aoife Rivera Serrano's translation."

—**Tace Hedrick,** professor, University of Florida, Gainesville, author of *Mestizo Modernism: Race, Nation and Identity in Latin American Culture, 1900–1940.* (Rutgers University Press, 2003).

Insularismo

Antonio S. Pedreira

An Insight into the Puerto Rican Character

Insu-lar-ismo

Foreword by Nicolás Kanellos, Ph.D.
Translated by Aoife Rivera Serrano

Ausubo Press
New York City

For information, address
Ausubo Press
130 Seventh Avenue
New York, NY 10011-1803

A CIP catalog record for this book is available from the Library of Congress.

ISBN 1-932982-40-X

Design by Stephanie Tevonian

Contents

Insular **ismo**

Foreword

*t*here has never been a more influential book or treatise on Puerto Rican culture than Antonio Pedreira's *Insularismo*. The mature product of the rapid political and cultural changes experienced by Puerto Ricans as they passed from one colonial master to another in the early twentieth century, *Insularismo* sought to plumb the depths and intra-history of Puerto Rican conscience by addressing the educational, moral, aesthetic and social problems of Puerto Ricans. By the time Pedreira had penned his landmark book-length essay in 1934, he had already renewed Puerto Rican letters and opened up new avenues for the forging of a Puerto Rican national identity in four previous books examining the history of the island and its relationship to old- and new-world cultures: *De los nombres de Puerto Rico* (1927), *Aristas* (1930), *Hostos, Ciudadano de América* (1931) and *Bibliografía puertorriqueña* (1932). His decades-long engagement with the definition of Puerto Rican identity also included his editorship of *Indice* magazine and scores of newspaper columns in the popular press. Pedreira went on to write another handful of books and some 200 articles and essays for diverse periodicals.

It was with *Insularismo*, however, that Pedreira became the leader of the generation of writers who would dominate the intellectual circles of the island from the 1930s through the 1950s. Pedreira's approach to nonfiction writing as well as his incisive prose style led writers away from the poetic and impressionistic—even worse, bombastic and outlandish—essays of the immediate past and onto expository writing more based on research, documentation

and analysis; he earned respect for the essay as a genre of serious intellectual query as well as literary art. Pedreira proved that the genre could provide information while assisting in the construction of a national history and cultural identity.

This is not to say that *Insularismo* does not go overboard on the speculative; to the contrary, many of its premises and assertions about race, ethnicity and colonialism have been challenged by today's scholars, who attribute Pedreira's prescriptions and conclusions more to his own race and class interests than to impartial, social scientific observation and clear understanding of the new capitalist world formed after World War I and the imperial grip of the United States on the island.

While Pedreira's and *Insularismo*'s impact among recognized artists and intellectuals on the island cannot be doubted—they may be characterized as pre- and post-*Insularismo*—it is not clear just what impact Pedreira's thought had on working-class artists and writers, many of whom became economic refugees and had to migrate to New York, where they published their own working-class and racially sensitive interpretations of Puerto Rican culture and identity. Whereas Pedreira and his followers were enjoying the security and celebrity of island canonization at the very time when Puerto Rican nationalism was responding to United States hegemonic pressures, the racialized and economically disadvantaged classes of Puerto Rico were embarking on their own flesh-and-blood experiment in building a cultural identity, one to be forged out of uprootedness from traditional life, economic and power relationships; a separation and even severing of the linguistic and cultural bonds of their families and communities; two concepts of race and ethnicity in conflict from island to mainland; and, of course, classicism and marginalization in both island and continental spaces.

Inasmuch as the majority of Puerto Ricans never truly engaged in the debates engendered by *Insularismo*, but most of the people, in one form or another, directly or indirectly experienced the rapid socioeconomic transformation of Puerto Rico under United States colonial administration, and the emigration to the continent that it occasioned, *Insularismo*'s legacy must be examined once and for all by considering its impact on such working-class stateside writers as Jesús and Joaquín Colón, and the Nuyoricans who followed them in the sixties and seventies, for instance, not just the elites whose works became canonized on the island during the years subsequent to the publication of *Insularismo*.

Undoubtedly, this first and only translation of *Insularismo* will lead to such inquiry and evaluation and spark new debates as to Puerto Rican identity, now that Puerto Ricans are acknowledged as being bilingual and bicultural and the Puerto Rican diaspora has spread throughout the entire United States.

— *Nicolás Kanellos, Ph.D.*
Brown Foundation Professor
University of Houston, 2005

Preface

*i*translated *Insularismo* into English for the children of Puerto Ricans in the United States and other Latinos who can no longer negotiate the rococo Spanish written by the benchmark critic of his generation, Antonio S. Pedreira, in the Puerto Rico of the 1930s. Scholars and students of Latin American history will recognize the bewildering issues he raised that are yet to be settled in the Caribbean island. In this unique, discordant but pivotal Puerto Rican work, Pedreira aired the dirty laundry that still needs ventilating today. His unsparing criticism was inspired by a profound love for his people and his island and a deep frustration, a frustration he hoped would be relieved by the next generation, to whom he dedicated the last chapter.

As a Puerto Rican who frequently travels all over Latin America and visits family on the island twice a year, I can say without equivocation no generation since Pedreira's has faced his music. My hope is that those of us who now speak English as a first language will join Pedreira and objectively probe his polemical subjects regarding identity within Latin America, culture salvaging, and our inexorably mixed racial legacy.

In his own prologue, Pedreira refers to persistent problematic questions that robbed his peace of mind and that his countrymen were facing at the time. These questions had given rise to *Insularismo*, an admittedly subjective and personal historical interpretation he hoped would begin a process of fruitful introspection *that would lead to solutions*. In translating this book into English my hope, seventy-one years later, is the same.

— *Aoife Rivera Serrano, 2005*

Introduction

*a*fter the United States invaded Puerto Rico in 1898, the island's intellectual elite sought to find a deterrent to the engulfing process of Americanization by affirming the existence of a distinctly Puerto Rican personality and, by extension, a distinctive culture worthy of protection. The collective effort to curb cultural immersion found its most controversial expression in the work of writer and educator Antonio S. Pedreira (1899–1939), particularly in his influential *Insularismo*, first published in 1934. Written for an audience of intellectuals, and originally serialized beginning in 1929 in the Puerto Rican magazine *Indice, Insularismo* was not created for the average reader. Expressions in French, Italian and Latin are sprinkled here and there much like James Joyce did in his work. Names of intellectuals and artists of that era are also dropped throughout the text with the expectation that readers will immediately recognize the reference. Today, it is an anachronistic text, especially in English, but one that captures a moment in Puerto Rican history when questions of national identity and culture were being raised. In general I have maintained the essays' declamatory, turgid style to reflect Pedreira's tendentious invective and properly frame his ideas regarding race and national identity. A rendering of *Insularismo* in exclusively succinct, contemporary English, though the safest option for a translator, would compromise the book's value as an indicator of Latin American rhetoricalness. It would also eliminate the Puerto Rican discourse (or discursiveness) of the 1930s, as well as the idiosyncrasies of the author.

Suffering from the same despair that affected his contemporaries regarding the fate of Puerto Rico, Pedreira attempted to reconstruct the evolution of the Puerto Rican character by considering and speculating on historical fact, geographical data and behavioral tendencies. Pedreira's prologue, "Readers' Compass to *Insularismo*," foreshadowed his decidedly speculative approach, warning the reader that he pulled no punches in discussing his country or his compatriots. He insisted that only an "unadulterated"—that is to say severely critical—interpretation of the past would help set a future course for the nation. Accordingly, though Pedreira underscored the importance of the fateful political disruptions in the island's history, he posed the Puerto Rican character itself as the primary source of the country's dilemma: its inability to decide who and what it was, given its European, African and indigenous Taíno history and its then new relationship with the United States. In his biting critique of the Puerto Rican character, Pedreira departed from his contemporaries by posing the racial composition of the Puerto Rican character as one of the root causes of its "vacillation and irresolution." This paradigm shift fanned the flames of discourse and was best responded to in 1935 by historian and essayist Tomás Blanco in his books, *Prontuario Histórico de Puerto Rico* (A Compendium of Puerto Rican History) and *El prejuicio racial en Puerto Rico* (Racial Prejudice in Puerto Rico) in 1942.

Pedreira's beliefs in a determinism of the soul and in a geographic and biological determinism that was explicitly racist and sexist are well documented in his acerbic conclusions in the section entitled "Biology, Geography, Soul." Racial mixing, which Pedreira concludes was a typically Spanish weakness, bred feelings of superiority and inferiority that led to resentment, envy, hatred, and ultimately created paralyzing divisions among the people as a whole.

As to Pedreira's observations about women, there is no reasonable defense. They do, however, reflect the very irresolution and ambiguity he attributed to the Puerto Rican people. Accordingly, he warns the reader in his own prologue: "Internal contradictions...born from the very dynamics of the problem I endeavor to understand run through...[my] observations." Though he makes chauvinist remarks where women are concerned, he also extols them in the same breath, the same paragraph or on the same page. In the chapter called "Chess Table," for example, Pedreira referred to women's temperaments as "not having been emancipated from superficial concerns.... They are moved by the littlest things, and their nervous systems are easily triggered." Yet in the next sentence he declares, "I do not believe the braggart's silly propaganda about the inferiority of women. Neither do I believe in the traditional privileges of men that originate from social injustice...."

With regard to geography he believed the island's small size, isolation, and brutal heat, along with the hurricanes and tremors resulting from its geological features and location, helped to seal its fate and played a major role in forming the people's character. Yet Pedreira's primary concern was the psychological insularism he considered unique to Puerto Rico. It was derived, he believed, not only from the physical and climatological conditions peculiar to any people surrounded and cut off by water, but from a disadvantageous series of events that produced a systematized cultural subservience to Europe, and later to the United States.

In the section entitled "The Course of Our History," he touched upon what he considered the three definitive moments in the evolution of the Puerto Rican people: Spanish domination in the sixteenth century, the individualistic awakening in the nineteenth, and the unnerving instability of the twentieth. The period of initiation through the sixteenth century could not produce any distinguishing traits, according to Pedreira, since the indigenous element had been virtually eliminated. Spanish warfare in the seventeenth century distracted the declining European power and depleted its treasury. As a result Puerto Rico—neglected more than the other colonies—suffered immeasurably. The cultural stagnation of Spain during the eighteenth century had its impact on Puerto Rico as well, arresting the colony's intellectual development; in 1797, seven-tenths of the people were illiterate. In the late eighteenth and early nineteenth centuries, political upheaval in Spain profoundly affected its colonial possessions and in due course ignited the Puerto Rican imagination. In 1809 the first Puerto

Rican deputy to the Courts, Ramón Power, made a formal demand for rights and obtained the annulment of the absolute powers of the governors, in addition to other political reforms. Over the next nine decades there followed an independent press, literature by native authors, the abolition of slavery, the development of public education, the emergence of political parties and diverse popular movements. Puerto Rico's budding sense of patriotism coupled with political unrest in Cuba (where Puerto Ricans died in that country's fight for freedom) and Spain's fear of United States intervention in the Spanish Antilles finally produced the autonomy granted by Spain in 1897. However, the United States ultimately intervened in 1898, converting Puerto Rico into war booty by means of the Treaty of Paris. Puerto Rico's short-lived brush with independence was ended and Puerto Rico's fate was forever changed. Pedreira explains, "President McKinley checkmated the king of Spain and ever since then...our country finds itself in a tough period of transition, sandwiched as it is between two antithetical cultures."

Although Pedreira was troubled by the "sordid utilitarianism" and "rampant materialism" introduced by the new culture, he admonished the people to "get a firm and clear grip on...our moral frame and structure...and protect the body." He enthusiastically acknowledged that the invasion had transformed the island for the better insofar as industry, infrastructure, schools and greater freedoms were concerned, but he made clear that it had done so at an incalculable toll to the Puerto Rican psyche. Pedreira soberly put this transformation in perspective by pointing out the "inordinate increase in the number of bankruptcies, suicides, lunatics, criminals, TB cases, fraud, unskilled laborers and poor wretches in general." And with regard to the new language brought into his country, Pedreira criticized the North American attempt to unconscionably impose English-only instruction overnight in Puerto Rico. Pedreira preferred the learning of several languages with concentration on the mother tongue, Spanish, since the educator believed: "Language [was] the vault in which the embodiment of a people [was] deposited."

Pedreira found the exclusive and monopolizing nature of the

compulsory, English-only system to be intrinsically damaging and countereffective to learning of any kind since it completely disoriented and discouraged students. Nevertheless, he focused his criticism on the Puerto Rican movers and shakers who did not counteract the United States' educational process: a one size fits all approach that mirrored the mass production of United States industry. Education in the United States was designed for the masses, excluded the exceptional, and sustained the mediocre.

The list of topics that fell victim to Pedreira's pointed pen is long. Some readers may find it difficult to bear in mind that *Insularismo* was not an indiscreet or deliberately invidious exercise, but rather a product born from the crush of historical forces and, mostly, a labor of love.

Antonio Pedreira has been most widely and categorically criticized as a racist and Hispanophile, in spite of the fact that he recognized the work of poet Luis Palés Matos (a major exponent of Afro-Caribbean verse), authored the definitive biography of doctor and activist José Celso Barbosa (an identifiably black compatriot) and wrote books primarily about Puerto Rican subjects, for example, *El Periodismo en Puerto Rico* (Journalism in Puerto Rico), *El Año Terrible del 87* (The Terrible Year of '87) and *Bibliografía Puertorriqueña* (The Bibliography of Puerto Rico). In a Latin America where the population reflects the mix known as *la raza cósmica*, he is nonetheless regarded only as representative of his class and never as an individual vulnerable to the lethal combination of old-world hegemony, colonial dynamics and the historical pressures of the moment in which he lived. A more dispassionate view might consider that in light of the island's racial history, the author was likely a man of unidentifiable color who like many other Caribbeans struggled to come to terms with mixed feelings of self-hatred, self-acceptance and denial. He may have also been suffering from what has come to be called Latin American Fatalism. Indeed, the acrimonious melancholy and pessimism of his work express an internalized oppression, a colonization of the mind that many people of color under similar circumstances have been privy to, and which has found a voice in the characters of many writers, including James Baldwin and V. S. Naipaul. Similar issues of color in the former British Caribbean were historically and commonly operative in the lives of all West Indians.[1] Today this internalized conflict is noticeable in some Latin Americans and Latinos who still cling to a white identity that often confers status in their countries, better jobs and housing in the United States and—if they're fair-skinned enough—the privilege of hailing a cab in New York City. As in Pedreira's day, this deep-rooted dissonance continues to make us deaf to new ideas like those of Cornel West about color: Culture, not pigment per se, makes us brown.[2]

To read Pedreira is to believe that at one moment he loved his people and at another he loathed them. There is an estrangement and a fascination simultaneously at work here, an anguished analysis exacerbated by thirty-six years of the white/black dichotomy imported from the United States, which only served to entrench the defensive native color scale that had thirteen categories of skin color.[3] Puerto Rican sociologist Eduardo Seda attests to this entrenchment, ascertaining that Puerto Ricans suffer from "cryptomelanism," the fear of losing one's white identity in a new world order imposed by North American invaders. This dread is manifested by tenaciously hiding racial origins that in the United States can only fit a dual color code; you are either one or the other.[4]

To distill *Insularismo* exclusively through the filter of race, however, would extract a narrow interpretation of a book that turned out to be the catalyst for serious research on the content of Puerto Rican culture. Pedreira is the benchmark critic who remains one of the most frequently cited authors in any analysis regarding the ethos of the country. He is the leader of the "Generation of 1930" that so eagerly sought to discover the sum and substance of their culture. Speaking for himself and his compatriots Pedreira stated, "We sincerely believe that there is a Puerto Rican soul scattered, dispersed, in potentiality, luminously

---

[1] David Lowenthal, *West Indian Societies* (Oxford University Press, 1972).

[2] Cornel West, *The Cornel West Reader* (Basic Civitas Books, 1999).

[3] María Babín, *Panorama de la cultura puertorriqueña* (Biblioteca Puertorriqueña, 1958).

[4] *La Cultura política de Puerto Rico* (Ediciones Amauta, 1976).

fragmented like a frustrated puzzle that has never enjoyed the full sense of its wholeness."

This need for "wholeness" continues. In spite of a 107-year relationship with the United States, current-day Puerto Ricans cling to what remains of their cultural heritage and passionately discuss the contradictions of their political status. Both tendencies still reflect the spiritual state of affairs Pedreira spoke of years earlier in *Insularismo*. The persistence of this irresolution makes Pedreira's personal, unsparing, singularly Puerto Rican analysis of his country germane reading today as his compatriots, abroad and on the island, continue to question who they truly are, and intermittently vote to determine what they will become or, as Pedreira might have put it, *if* they will become.

— *Aoife Rivera Serrano, 2005*

Insular*ismo*

Insu-
lar-
ismo
1934

Readers' Compass to Insularismo

these pages will lack the admiring and complacent tone we have often taken when evaluating the reality of the Puerto Rican people. The text is not a product of scientific analysis. It is a response, free of dishonorable intentions, to a personal uneasiness rooted in the restlessness of the times, and arising from a series of events and attitudes subject to the most honest and impartial reflection.

I do not expect these observations, which seem valid to me, to be so to others. Internal contradictions and obvious repetitions born from the very dynamics of the problem I endeavor to understand may run through them. I write intuitively, searching for the secret significance of deeds marking the trajectory we have traveled as a people. Possible oversights that inevitably lead to erroneous conclusions have not escaped my attention. As I do not aim to create a historical, scientific or authoritative work on the basis of statistics, my personal reservations have been overcome by good intentions. These pages, then, do not pretend to resolve any problem, but rather to pose one. They constitute one of various positions that can be adopted with regard to a topic.

Eventually the essays answer the questions: All things considered, what are we on the whole? How are we different? I attempt to gather the dispersed elements beating at the heart of our culture and discover the salient characteristics of our collective psyche. Bear in mind that if it is difficult to define one single man because of the multiple facets that form his personality, it is much more difficult to define a people. The difficulty increases a degree when one attempts to define a group of human beings, as is this case, that have not yet been able to satisfactorily trace their collective life.

We have lived attached to an optimistic and baseless interpretation of our history from whence springs the arrogant flaw of believing ourselves to be the *ne plus ultra* of Antillean peoples. Enthusiastic followers of rhetorical patriotism, we have taken to skillfully concealing the pejorative interpretation of certain honest observations about Puerto Rico and its people. To discover the unadulterated truth about our psyche's spontaneous manifestations and uncover those underlying attitudes that certainly escaped the pen of unsuspecting government historians, one must carefully roam the outskirts of official history. From these peripheral excursions and those details unwittingly leaked through bureaucratic red tape, we should be able to arrive at conclusions about our unique character.

It is high time we do away with the self-serving idolatry that tends to characterize our personality. It is based on attained heights of perfection that have not yet gone beyond wishful thinking. We assert our virtues from habit as if we had truly fulfilled their measure. What we should be and what we want to be are quite far from what we have been and what we are now. Anyone concerned with defining an indefinable people who, in their delusions of grandeur, willfully conceal faults and failings from themselves and others, must compensate by highlighting their weaknesses to some extent. In this way they can be impartially judged in their proper context. Having provided for a margin of error, I allow the cheerful music that celebrates the tropics to drift away readily and without reservation, since it only exalts virtues that have not gone beyond the dream state.

Plaudits promote positive reinforcement, resistant conformity and vainglory. Pessimism and doubt are vital forces that drive one to examine one's conscience. Discussion clears reasoning and often stimulates reform. Rodó says, "...There is a pessimism that has the import of paradoxical optimism. Far from assuming a resigned and condemnatory attitude toward life it propagates, through its discontent with what exists, the need to reform it." The bitterness that may trickle through these essays is accompanied by hope for change.

To date, the bulk of our qualities is usually measured from the changeable perspective of politics. This vantage point has shifted according to the instability of its base. Our politics have tragically developed with an eye only toward greater profit and influence. The expedient, the advantageous, the obligatory: These have been the standards for all our political parties. We live and breathe politics. The unavoidable topic at work, in schools, theaters, newspapers, soirees and everywhere is invariably politics. We have as such developed an electoral approach for evaluating everything, and our perspective varies according to the circumstances. In the past, being a politician was a patriotic duty; today it is a profession. Compare the politics of the nineteenth century with the twentieth and the change in motivation will be evident: from that of rendering service to holding an office, from sacrificing to prospering, from striving to attaining. A spirit for social programs used to dominate, now it is personal interest with a special favor concealed in each undertaking. We need to retain the sum and substance of our politics, but refrain from using the rising tide and its last-minute ebb as a base for an impartial evaluation of the problems we tackle here. The earth's mantle may issue from the sea floor, but it is in flux nonetheless.

By the same token, the measure of our character cannot be taken if it is based on a comparison between progress under the dominion of one government or another. "Frivolous people," Ortega y Gasset says, "think that human progress consists of a quantitative increase in things and ideas. No, no. True progress lies in the growing fullness with which we understand half a dozen fundamental mysteries that at the dawn of history throbbed convulsively like indestructible hearts." Let us find out if those mysteries exist for us and what their meanings are. Or, at the least, let us try to unlock the essence of our character. In *La Agonía Antillana* (Antillean Agony), Araquistáin says with regard to Puerto Rico, "Overwhelmed as everyone is by political worries, there are few who have the leisure to concern themselves with the essence of things and of life." My wish is to delve into that essence.

Toward this goal of analytically recreating the structure of our character, we have had to hold at bay the constant exceptions that have surfaced, mainly attending to findings that can alter the rule. The complexity of the matter demands rejecting exceptions that by their number tend to make one skeptical about the need for synthesis. I well know, and even desire, that such rationalizations remain in the reader's mind to sow dissension. Had I merely desired to be agreeable, these pages would never have been written.

Since I have already pointed out the direction my interpretation shall take, it is also pertinent to clarify what I understand as culture. The comfortable but poor definition that makes culture an affair peculiar to knowledge or morality frequently masks simplistic reasoning. I believe along with Ludwig Pfandl that "...culture does not indicate the *suma* or *síntesis* of all intellectual and spiritual interactions, but rather the exterior world, the environment Carlos Justi eloquently called the ether of things." What I shall understand as culture is the repertoire of conditions that give tone to events and watershed moments in the lives of countries, their particular response to things—ways of conceiving and creating—that distinguishes one national group from another. Culture is more than progress; it is a vital force.

In order to reasonably define this universal rhythm and determine the formation of a Puerto Rican disposition within it, one does not have to lose sight of those areas of quantitative quality in which culture tends to divide itself: the universal, the national and the individual. Oswald Spengler, in his much discussed work *The Decline of the West*, divides the first into two great periods: ancient culture with an Apollonian soul and Western culture with a Faustian soul. Restlessness and serenity differentiate them. Within these extremes, Spain is no more than an attitude on the scale of Western culture and we, an American expression of Spain's culture.

And it is this aspect of our country that interests us. Despite reducing the complexity of the matter to such simple terms, grasping our nature is still difficult because we cannot disregard the Anglo-Saxon aspect that is today slowly seeping into our Hispanic soul by way of the United States.

I see three definitive moments in the development of our people. The first is a time of passive formation and merging, starting with the discovery and conquest and ending in the last years of the eighteenth century and first years of the nineteenth. The second is a period of awakening and beginning and closes with the Spanish American War. And the third, where we find ourselves now, is one of indecision and transition. In the beginning, we were nothing more than a faithful continuation of Spanish culture; in the second period we began to exhibit an independent streak; and in the third we have wanted to continue its development with the modification of another expression of Western culture, the Saxon, superimposed on the other two. I am not interested, for the time being, in discussing the results of this last graft, but in pointing out the disruption of our intrinsic evolution, which has never come to fruition.

We had an origin and we had growth, yet we never had a rebirth. We emerged from one influence and walked into another never having fully established our ethos, which we have not lost completely and is adrift at this historical moment. So this thing we consider our ethos without claiming its parity with the Spanish or Anglo-Saxon attitudes in Western culture but always acknowledging its subservience, for the time being, to the Spanish is what we have termed insularism and is our only reason for concern. The systematic conditions upon which it has been sustained historically are what here we will understand as Puerto Rican culture.

By the same token, if we isolate the concept of its international dependence, we immediately stumble upon the fact that the Spanish legacy is infinitely superior to what has been created. We have not created a language, an art form or a national philosophy. Like many other countries, we have lacked the benefit of the indigenous factor, an imposing interpretation of life's meaning, and the leap to the abstract that is proof of solidity and maturity as a

nation. Culturally we were and continue to be a Hispanic colony. And yet within the harmony of our people, a unique rhythm is emerging. If it indeed has not been able to manifest itself fully and in one burst, it has nevertheless been able to differentiate itself to some degree (as it has in other peoples) from the common order that Spain created in America.

Consider this a work in progress, a preliminary collection of ruminations and reflections intended to expand upon several facts I believe essential in defining the Puerto Rican people. Any piecemeal dissection will be detrimental to the whole. Do not expect remedies, for I am not a psychiatrist and so have none to offer. My purpose is rather to assemble the diverse elements that may help to make sense out of our character. I have written these personal essays in response to persistent questions that have robbed my peace of mind. They were woven together in the desire to abolish hypothetical rebirths. Instead of mending the country's tatters with threads of lamentation or patches of indifference, I propose that we scrupulously adorn her with a commitment to duty.

Ultimately this book attempts to examine the essential rhythms that we follow. Upon doing a general survey of literature to write this prologue, many undeveloped ideas caught my attention. They are like newly planted seeds waiting for the reader to make them burst forth.

I make use of the essay form because it is a flexible genre where many things are begun and few are concluded.

—Antonio S. Pedreira, 1934

Biology, Geography, Soul

The People and Their Significance

according to our first historian, Iñigo Abbad, when European blood baptized indigenous *Boriquén* with Christianity, "the island, under the command of Juan Ceron in 1509, was as populated with Indians as a beehive and so beautiful and fertile that it looked like an orchard." From their primitive organization our peasants inherited the *bohío* [a hutlike dwelling], the hammock, the earthen jar, and the *higüera* [an eating or serving utensil made from a gourd of the same name], but our peasants did not inherit the fierce, warring independence that launched the Indians upon risky expeditions outside of *Boriquén*. In 1511 the aborigines who could not submit to the conquistadors revolted and in a few years their numbers were reduced considerably by exploitation and disease.

To counteract this loss and their unsuitability for strenuous work, the Royal Order of 1513 introduced the African element to the island. The black man did the work of four and with the introduction of slavery, this third ethnological type became part of our racial composition, creating one of our great social problems. In time their plight provokes strong objections in our growing collective consciousness, and unceasing efforts on their behalf. The Spanish element founds our country and it fuses with the other races. Out of this fusion our con-fusion is born.

Insular*ismo*

Gradually exterminated by plague and subjugation, the fusing indigenous race stops being a major factor in the racial mixture some years after the conquest, leaving two races with contradictory roots and dispositions face to face. The superior race provided intelligence and planning, and the so-called inferior race reluctantly contributed the work. Both had traits that were difficult to reconcile. Between the two the distance that separates the free man from the slave, the civilized from the barbaric, the European from the African intervened. The white race decreed; the black carried out the decree. One imposed the project and ruled; the other lent his brawn and obeyed. While the European owned lives and land, the African had no right to even determine his or her own feelings. Neither did he worry or think about anything, since the ruling race did the thinking for all, maintaining for itself a moral hold over the whole. Today, a large part of the Puerto Rican masses is indentured, their innermost sense of personal liberty still held in pledge; it is at the root of our character.

These two main pillars preserved their racial purity during the first days of colonization, the barrier between them maintained by the contempt the European felt toward the African and the resentment the latter felt for his owner. Barriers and feelings of animosity, however, were overcome. Spanish scrupulousness gave in to one of their characteristic overindulgences that subscribed to the principle: The race that founds becomes fused and con-fused. The colonizers divided themselves into clear social lots including at its highest level nobility, governors and those with titles; and at its lowest end the people, and soldiers whose obligations, rights and privileges were quite dissimilar. Though it is true the first group wanted to maintain the purity of their blood at all cost since it guaranteed them privileges, honors and membership into the most exclusive echelons of society, it is no less true that the plebeian whites were not as conscientious in maintaining their social stratification and little by little started to mix with the black race, whose population has never outnumbered the white.

In the eighteenth century, when the already declining indigenous population is almost completely snuffed out, there remained the white and black ethnological factors exclusively at work, adding to the cross-breeding from which the *mestizo* resulted.

Two antagonistic races wrestled within the *mestizo* in a difficult union of clashing cultures. Between the superior and inferior races stands the mulatto, who will always belong to a fringe group with both racial dispositions, one of which will grow depending on whom he chooses for a subsequent pairing: *mestizo*, white or black. The mulatto, a combination of the latter two and generally not one thing or the other, is at bottom undefined and wavering, in conflict, maintaining both racial dispositions without ever defining himself socially. He lives for the moment, defending himself from everyone, including himself, without breaking rules or making waves. He is prudent but indecisive, like a man who finds himself caught in the fire between two warring camps. To resolve their situation they need a more pronounced measure of one racial camp or the other. Blacks belong to a group that participates but does not create, that follows but does not initiate, that marches in file but does not lead the parade. Generally, he lacks the fervor to be a leader.

From the coupling of full-blooded Spaniards who were futilely waging a losing battle on the island against disease and the climate, the *criollo* was born, somewhat pale and agile, and after some generations able to assimilate and make the most of the rigors of the tropics. The great mass of peasants largely come from here, men of excellence who by dint of their struggle with inclement Nature have developed physical constitutions almost immune to the same diseases that wreaked such havoc upon the first Europeans. It is awesome to consider our humble farmer, this *criollo*, this *jíbaro*, bent over a hoe from sun to sun, his life exposed to the elements, battered by deprivation and hookworm, yet always enduring despite a deficient diet. He is a fellow who also lives for the present, who works out of necessity, who resorts to gambling in order to gather in a moment the resources he thinks are impossible to obtain with persistent work. Generous and courteous, hospitable and fun-loving, he has had to find refuge in shrewdness to protect himself from being tyrannized by city slickers and competitors from the black provinces on the coast. Our *jíbaro* is by nature mistrusting and shy and although benevolent to his own, suspicious and astute. Fed up with unkept promises and proposals laid aside, he has had to fall back on his keen mind to put a stop to the fraud and excesses of the city. Our *criollo* poet Luis Lloréns Torres was able to masterfully touch upon this despair and mistrust when in a burst of precise psychological profiling he wrote this ten-line stanza:

> A *jíbaro* arrived in San Juan
> And a couple of no-nothing *yanquis*
> Cut short his walk in the park;
> They wanted to win him over.
> They spoke to him of Uncle Sam,
> Of Wilson, of Mr. Root,
> Of New York, of Sandy Hook,
> Of liberty, of the vote,
> Of the dollar, of habeas corpus
> And the *jíbaro* said: Uh-huh.[5]

A philosophical reading of the *jíbaro* has not yet been done and this is not the occasion to waste time doing so. When it is attempted, his virtues, defects and unique approach to facing life will have to be highlighted.

Well, then, the *criollo* and the mulatto have become perfectly acclimated to our soil. The latter, who carries African stamina in his blood, upon coupling again with the black produced another intermediate type, the *grifo*, who has more robust constitution and effrontery than any other product of Puerto Rican ethnology, and who has been taking over the rugged work of our coasts and sugar mills. Quick-witted and agile, the strength of the black and the intelligence of the white prevail in him, but are never well-balanced. When we hear someone in a bilious fit of temper use that so common phrase "uppity *grifo*," both characteristics are being underscored in the insult. The *grifo* fights decidedly and vehemently from the deepest part of his soul for full recognition of his

---

[5]Antonio Pedreira and Concha Meléndez, "Luis Lloréns Torres, el poeta de Puerto Rico," *RABA*, XLVII (1933), núm. 115.

abilities and for the egalitarian treatment that will ensure his share of opportunities in life. Subconsciously he feels compelled to revindicate the slave. The mulatto is not as determined to seek so much. He is too agreeable to be pulled by one side or another. Yet the *grifo*, bolstered by that portion of white blood that guarantees his rights, aspires and has ambitions. His resentments find an escape valve in democracy. Since he tends to put himself on the same level as the white man, at times he is prepared for the fight. At other times his preparation is a sham and casts doubt on his self-proclaimed equality, so that in some cases he proves to be a promising individual, in others a questionable one.

When one of these individuals is able to break from this prevailing stereotype, he usually rises very high and obtains the respect and affection that he deserves due to his exceptional qualifications. We are obligated to lovingly include all groups that are genuinely worthy, without feeding that horrible beast called social prejudice. Consider that within a great percentage of our population, the prototypes do not remain separate in clear lots, but are solidly established in each person, in such a way that the characteristic traits of each type are thoroughly blended and dissolved in the white man's crucible, the point of departure almost completely erased.

In these indistinct cases atavism works so slowly that no one would suspect the existence of a biological civil war in certain members of the genealogical tree. Here is the no-man's-land of our social life and a new reason to maintain a tactful cordiality beneficial to all.

One may even include a discussion of the *grifo*'s opposite type and other subgroups whose differentiation could take us quite far. If this attempt at classification would be taken to its furthest limit, additional observations would make our reasoning more evident. But it is not necessary to press the issue. Our effort will limit itself to indicating the three racial dispositions that are basic to our psychology, and the two or three primary derivations that arise from their mix.

Leaving aside the erstwhile indigenous element because of its shrinking population, the black and white along with their odd, mixed offspring should give us a great deal to think about in terms of our incomprehensible collective psychology. During the eighteenth century, Friar Iñigo Abbad certainly saw the problem when he said in reference to us: "It is true that if you look at them as a whole, without thinking about it, little difference is noticeable in their traits and you can only detect a people as mixed and ambiguous-looking as all their colors." In the same manner, our psychology is mixed up and ambiguous.

Deep down within each of us we will find a phlegmatic biological battle between scattered and antagonistic forces that have retarded the definitive formation of our character. The master and peon who live in each of us is not able to temper the harshness each feels for the other, and we saddle our identity as landed gentry with the sad condition of tenant farmers. The determination and disposition of the European and the doubt and resentment of the African stand side by side. In the most difficult moments our decision making is erratic, shuttling and searching restlessly for its destination. Our rebellions are momentary, our passivity permanent. During times of historical significance when the marshaling rhythms of our European ancestors flower in our gestures, we are capable of great undertakings and the most courageous heroism. Yet when the impulse comes steeped in African blood we hesitate, as if left agape before colorful beads, or frightened before the cinematic image of witches and ghosts.

We are a difficult people to please since we are difficult to comprehend. I do not assert that everything is a result of our diverse roots and racial mixing, but that a point of departure for interpreting our "very mixed and ambiguous" character is noting how differently we respond to the secret biological stimuli within us. These repugnant forces exhausting themselves in incessant, invisible clashes blur the panorama of our aspirations. A nebulous storm sweeps through our confused objectives, hurling each one to the side, barring us from gathering ourselves in an impregnable front before history. Some men called leaders, with only the airs of statesmen, change political programs overnight, unite us to, and separate us from parties with opposing platforms, while we remain docile with the classic meekness of the lamb on our royal coat of arms. The indigenous blood still running through our veins rears its head for an instant, only to be suffocated by the impulse of the conquistador or the slave. The result is a tropical laissez faire, a people in wait of a better opportunity, and while we wait we quietly submit, always coming up with excuses.

The problem is that there does not exist among us a commonality of interests, emotions and ideas. Cursed with what Rafael María de Labra called Antillean particularism, and which for us is inherited, we lack a sense of cooperation and proportion. Hence it is relatively easy to disrespect an entire people whose principal weakness rests on an inability to unite and act selflessly. When the white man protests, the black gives in and vice versa—will the ironic implication here be understood?— without ever managing to arrive at a oneness of purpose. Instead, harmony is achieved by reaching superficial understandings with servile accommodations to all situations in an effort to appease and cease fire on opposing forces. The respite is, naturally, short-lived; the best way of not pleasing anyone is to try to please everyone.

As a result of events past and present, we have developed considerable proficiency for assimilating, which in the Hispanic race has determined the course of its progress. Said assimilation in Spain would operate over a body of people strong and defined, but in our case over a graft of people within whom are others who are irresolute and ill defined. We lacked the autochthonous base necessary to compensate for the effects of foreign contributions. We have had to form the bedrock of our history with contributions alien to our indigenous territorial spirit. Since the indigenous factor did not exercise a conditioning influence, we remained passive and obedient before the dictating voice of the outlander. The result was submission, humility, conformity, diffidence, the loyal meekness that set the tone for our development. "Culture and civilization, which make us so vain," Ortega y Gasset said, "are the creation of the savage, not the educated and civilized man." If the value of primitive society is that of being the wellspring of cultural and civil organization, we have not had that wellspring. Everything came handed down to us and ready made, and so our people became accustomed to consumption, not to the creation of vital, essential values.

Obey, defer, accept: these are symptomatic reactions. We begin by accepting historic designs without considering the remote possibility of changing their pattern. We end by obeying the imperious voice of their excellencies, the military governors who until the end of the past century made us obey them with the rude dictum "My wish is your command." That attitude has not changed to this day.

In a matter of speaking, cockfighting sheds some light on who we are. Our national sport is not a pastime exclusively our own. Nevertheless it seems as if it were made for us; it is a sport where, unlike Spanish bullfighting, individual stakes are not high. Coordinated teamwork like that found in British soccer or North American baseball is not found here either. We strip ourselves of all responsibility and allow the cocks to resolve the situation. This way no one will doubt our ability for joint action. In the cocks' ring—as in our folk songs—we vent some of the congested impulses that seethe inside us and once more divide the insular uproar into two opposing camps. The cockfighting game is more the sphere of old men than young now, and it is sharing its overriding popularity with new sports.

I am haunted by the picture of youngsters who hardly experience their youthfulness. In tropical countries people age much faster than in cold countries. Moreover, life expectancy is shorter in the former than in the latter. Our children hurriedly pass through the very phase in which they should be delighting. Their eyes are opened too soon, the best years of their childhood wasted before their time. With dismaying frequency we see them abandon the games appropriate for their age to dedicate themselves to work, and sex diverts their attention before puberty sets in.

Just as the infantile tantrum is expected in the child, the entrance of a young man into public life is also expected, encumbering the course of his growth and character. His inability to impose his own will due to his young years obliges him to back the opinions of others, and life's whirlwind drags him down, a legion of woes crushing his spirit. In the vegetable patches of our fields, in the belly of a factory, in an office or on an unemployment line, he starts to live out an insipid experience without ever savoring the legitimate years of his youth.

This rush to be men is inherited from our ancestors. Compare the student body of our university with a similar one in the United States, and see the difference between young men and old boys. Our average student lives out his college years acrimoniously, defends his rights with vigorous protest, does not enjoy the summer of his youth and leaves the classroom embittered without ever harboring a loving memory of his alma mater. The North American never forgets his alma mater because he passed the best years of his youth within her walls. If he ever stood up in protest it was for a sports event, a case of high jinks at best.

Renouncing one's youth ahead of time is denying our people the sound health, vigor and joy that youth should give them. Due to a series of circumstances in which ethnology, geography and history all play a part, we are a sad people. Campeche, Oller, Gautier Benítez, Juan Morel Campos, first-rate painters, poets and musicians, were the most expressive vehicles of Puerto Rican sadness. When you consider the dimensions of a land besieged by earthquakes and storms and by taxes; when you grasp the impotence of the people in waging a losing battle with their biological makeup and their political tragedy, when you consider the landscape or hear the sorrowful melodies of our measured, rhythmic *danza*; when, finally, you look deep into our foundations, worn away by so many impediments, you can discover the old sources of our melancholy.

Puerto Rico is a depressed nation, but she loves life and never gives up. The native Puerto Rican is individualistic, tenacious, brave. Hunger does not faze him; faced with natural disasters, he is never undone. As an individual he will risk his life for any personal trifle without a care; collectively he is the opposite. He shows a marked inability to die in a group. Contrary to other Antillean peoples, ours is greatly attached to life. The *areyto*, an indigenous tune originating in the Dominican Republic, states, "*Ijí, ayá bombé*" (death before servitude). A contempt for life characterizes both the Dominican and Cuban peoples who, to the astonishment of all, at any given moment risk it. In contrast, our common people are docile and passive; they are characterized by resignation. They defend their right to live with extreme wariness and demonstrate an instinctive prudence that some identify with fear. I beg the easily offended reader not to brush aside this analysis with overly celebrated exceptions.

We are a racially heterogeneous people, made up of white, black and *mestizo*. Centuries of living together at a tropical boiling point gradually produced marriages of contradictory ways and although divorces abound, our collective personality is responsible for a handful of names that represent us in almost every aspect of island culture.

To foreign armies we have given illustrious names like Rius Rivera y Pachín Marín, better men than Antonio Valero de Bernabé; to hagiography a distinguished woman, Santa Rosa de Lima; to juridical sciences, Eugenio María de Hostos; to the seas, Ramón Power and the pirate Cofresí; to botany, Stahl; to engineering, Fuertes; and in medicine, teaching, oratory, in arts and letters we have had names of considerable prestige. When I ask myself about patriotic distinction, I name Baldorioty to the place of honor; when I look for integrity I find it in Ruiz Belvis or Betances; a philosophical mind, Matienzo or López Landrón; a journalist, Salvador Brau or Muñoz Rivera.

My sympathies, as this first essay closes, go directly to that splendid anonymous mass formed by thousands of silent, steadfast and upright individuals who with admirable civic bearing—decency, selflessness, patriotism—daily contribute, unwittingly, to molding the Puerto Rican character. If this trailblazing minority has cleared the way to immortality so that others in our country may pass, it will also be the stronghold from which our eminent citizens are catapulted toward their places in the world.

Let us now take our leave of the people and their significance in order to posit my opinion of the land.

The Land and Its Significance

In this quest to make biological and political sense out of our ways, we find that geography and climate contribute greatly to devitalizing the people. The Indian defended his right to live with a minimum of effort, demanding very little in return. Accustomed to this effortless way of life, his exposed body could not bear the hardship of strenuous labor. The black man, subject to the lash, repressed his basic needs with obligatory Christian resignation. During the classic midday siesta the white man made his indolence all the more pleasant and leisured, soothing himself with the swaying motion of the hammock he inherited from the Indian. Nature's bounty and the fertile land provided generously for his daily needs. The climate called for little clothing and simple housing, with the land providing all else, but when the exigencies of colonial life began to strip the soil of its productive capacity, a mountain of troubles arose, historical millstones that we have dragged along to this very day.

Along with our political and psychological defects, our geographical location causes us to live in a continuous state of anxiety, anticipating destructive summer hurricanes and, at any moment, the dreaded earthquakes. Tremors and storms astound us with their desolating power, and so we live in constant watch for these

21

inevitable natural disasters. Regularly threatened by nature, our harvests poor due to droughts or inclement rains, we have had to live in apprehension and despair, beset by bad soil and defeat. Our main crops, sugarcane, tobacco and coffee are violently affected by the uneven climate, forcing the landowner to think about his failure daily. This defeatist attitude is at work in our general passivity and is at the heart of our pessimism.

The climate dissolves our will, rapidly and adversely affecting our psyche. The heat ripens us ahead of time and ahead of time it withers us as well. Weighed down by its debilitating effects, the people developed the national characteristic we call *aplatanamiento*, a term derived from the word "plantain." In our country this refers to a kind of inhibition stemming from mental lassitude and a lack of aggressiveness. It means following stolidly, comfortably and routinely the course of daily life without changes, free from anxieties, napping instead of aspiring, sitting idly by instead of rising to face the future. It means acclimating oneself to the enervating balm of the tropics and passively ruminating over ideas that take the shape of snow cones to cool the siesta of our complacency. *Musa paradisiaca*, the ineffable and scientific name for the plantain, is a rhetorical symbol for our vegetative state of mind.

Despite the consistent temperatures of a tropical climate our island has a few stimulating variations. Climatological differences have been recorded between day and night proportionately greater than the differences between one season and another.

The variability of our climate and the extreme differences between the north and south are noteworthy given the small stretch of 3,860 square miles of land in Puerto Rico, with cold, damp north and northeasterly winds from November to February and hot, dry southerly winds particularly from July to October. In the parched and calcined Ponce region, stunted grass cries out for artificial irrigation, trying to grow despite its arrested and desperate condition. A layer of dust covers great stretches of land that here and there, as if by a miracle, are devoted to cattle raising. In the north, rains are heavy and unexpected and keep the arable land in picturesque expectation of photographers and tourists. The interior towns,

Aibonito and Adjuntas, some 2,000 feet above sea level, offer our low barometric pressure a pleasing summer retreat. The average temperature is seventy-three degrees during the cold months and seventy-nine during the hot months. The yearly average is seventy-six degrees. Quick and sudden rains accumulate at a yearly average of 69.30 inches but do not last long.

Visitors fix their bucolic observations upon the rustic parts of the island. Drawings and multicolored prints of the landscape define us and, like good tourists, they prefer the picturesque to the essential. They are deaf to the clamor of landowners who, overwhelmed by the economic stranglehold of corporations, surrender their inheritance day by day. The visitor sees only the backdrop that diverts attention from our real tragedy. The land is slipping out of our hands without our even noticing, and the forests have disappeared by the power of the ax, leaving plains in their stead and hills stripped of trees by merciless deforestation. The fifty rivers that refresh us are dwindling in volume and the farmer is losing, year after year, the ownership of his orchards. Puerto Rico's agrarian nature has changed appreciably in appearance, consistent with the dictates of economic pressures we will discuss later.

Our geological structure, mounted in the air between two abysses—one to the south of the island at a depth of 15,000 feet and another seventy-five miles to the north and 28,000 feet deep—is poor in mineral resources. Little by little, native woods have also disappeared and our current shortage of mahogany, *ausubo* and *ortegón* is deplorable. Our stateliest and sturdiest trees have given way to prettier more decorative ones such as the pine and cypress. Deforestation is responsible for spindling rivers and a declining bird population. Puerto Rico is home to 160 species of birds, numbering about thirty in each town; we have fewer birds than any other Caribbean island because our cage is too small.

Our landscape is temperate and in harmony with our geography and ethnography. No power, no pomp, no magnitude. The discreet decor is low key and lends itself, as our *danza*, to modest pleasures and intimacy. Its predominant note is lyrical: delicate, mild, voluptuous, crystalline. Samuel Gili Gaya captured the land very well when he said, "It is far from imposing. Everything about it takes on an obliging air of mellowness, brightness, benevolence and a profound femininity. The mountains are nothing more than hills cloaked in bright green, where a cow grazes so peacefully, it seems more vegetable than animal. Upon first sighting, the land almost seems to threaten, but quickly regrets its killer appearance and inclines itself with much courtesy before the cobalt blue of the southern coast. We notice the absence of poisonous serpents and we cannot believe in the hurricanes and earthquakes that are said to occur."

Neither do we find within our island inaccessible peaks, burning deserts, steep precipices, the roar or paw prints of wild beasts in a wild land. We are strangers to violence and politely placid like our landscape. Isolated in rural zones, 80 percent of the population tends toward a meekness verging on indigence, and they increasingly aggravate their pressing socioeconomic problems by fathering children out of wedlock. The obligatory exodus to the cities is depriving the Puerto Rican landscape of any semblance of its traditional way of life. The great surge in sugar cane plantations went uphill, beyond the plains and slopes, knocking down trees and razing the minor crops that were dietary staples in the dreary homes of our farmers. The growth of sugar cane plantations has wiped out the native *bohío*, as well as swamps, brush, haciendas, mills and the original dirt roads. During the current period of veritable transition we are experiencing, the landscape continues to change its constitutive parts just the same as History is doing.

Here and there thick columns of black smoke darken the diaphanous blue sky, and an impressive network of roads, white over green, grips the muscular mountains, tightly joining seventy-eight towns and over forty sugar mills. From bend to bend a blaring announcement, a sales pitch from a peddler of exotic goods, pierces the fumes of molasses and gasoline that often compete with those of clandestine stills. The land is worked with forced enthusiasm and little, if any, return for the hand that tills it. Telegraph and electric wires streak the countryside like a musical score; technical progress is starting to invade rural zones in leaps and bounds, villages stretch outward, and distances almost reduced to nothing are shortened further by the impressive network of communications. Our landscape has acquired an urban character never dreamed of thirty years ago. Its face has been changed favorably by the number of farms, rural schools, sprinkler systems, secondary roads, automobiles, radios, etc. Yet the land continues in decline, absorbing social and economic ills that put pressure now, as before, on the problem of our national character.

With the exceptions of England, Java, Belgium and the Netherlands, our country has the densest population in the world, 485 inhabitants to the square mile, followed by Japan and Germany. If the population doubles every forty-five years, as the last censuses indicate, and if it continues gravitating toward this excessive number the problems of society, health and the economy that today overwhelm us will be even more frightening in the near future. Poor in minerals, woodlands and the hydraulic power needed to start up permanent industry, the land cannot support an already unnerving overpopulation.

From Columbus' ship the first man to spot land in the new world cried the first Spanish word America heard, one that prefigured a serious Puerto Rican problem, *"¡Tierra!"* ("Land ho!") Said land, no longer a cause for so arduous an expression of joy, turned into a cause for pain and anguish. The land, previously distributed in small plots, today is found in the grip of large sugar mills. Competition sinks its teeth into our sick economy and lowers the price of a day's wages, bringing the worker to the brink of indigence. Add the scourges of Mother Nature, hookworm, single-crop farming and periods when the soil cannot be tilled, and it is clear that the land can no longer bear so great a burden.

At the present time, neither immigration nor birth control, so evidently contrary to the Puerto Rican character, is helping. As we cannot reduce the number of births or spread outward because of the sea, we have no recourse but to expand vertically, go upward, inward and downward in order to cultivate ideas and a sense of purpose. Not to grow culturally condemns us to the unpleasant status of peons. We must therefore defend our spiritual subsoil—never forgetting her!—yet look upward away from the land to ensure for our people the air they breathe.

The geographical position of Puerto Rico determined the course of our history and our character. The concern of the Spanish sovereign was commercial, of the North American, strategic. Commerce and military tactics intervened in the development of our collective personality, as we shall see later. But the last straws added to this desperate situation were those of being isolated and of being the smallest of the large Antilles. Both deprived us of the authority to demand the respect accorded to great multitudes of people. Our country has always yearned for that land mass so necessary to serving as a foundation.

Puerto Rico's wealth developed in proportion to its dimensions, and so did its culture. Since the island was between the two Americas, and because it was small, lacked ports and large-scale commerce, it became a small patch of land in a remote corner of the world. Though a geographical hub, we are so cramped as to be good for nothing more than a military strategic location and as a way station, and this so seldom and briefly it does not foster an environment for definitive collaborations. Being a strategic point benefits us very little. As a tourist spot our small island does not compensate for the expense of the trip because it can be seen in two days. And as a financial center its geographical length only permits small-scale business deals, consistent with its size.

We are handicapped by our territorial dimensions. We are not continentals or even Antilleans. We are simply islanders, which is to say insulated and isolated in a narrow house. Drawn inward by the land, our outlook on the world takes on the same qualities. No deserts, no wide, open plains or deep valleys to help us expand our vision. We are used to tripping over the four corners of a landscape we stumble upon almost immediately. The impediment of such immediacy narrows our perspective and develops in us a myopia that condemns us to merely glimpsing the continent.[6] What we

---

[6] Vide "The Dutchman Will Catch Us" on page 92.

envisage for ourselves is limited, and our lives are diminished with serious consequences for our collective destiny.

The land then reduces the size of the stage wherein the culture is to move. Had our topography been different the course of our history similarly would have been different. Puerto Rico could not retain the likes of Ruiz Belvis, Hostos and Betances. They fled to die in exile. Our eminent men, it must be repeated, lacked that land mass so propitious for advancing and sharpening the faculties of historical figures. This geological insufficiency together with our troublesome geographic position and enervating climate, our biological makeup and our perpetual feudatory state all work to depress and inhibit our collective psyche. Lacking the right of might, that is, of the masses, we have not been able to incorporate into our life the power that confers rights. Our people have always been unlucky, poor and withered; we function in the diminutive. As a substitute for the inaction of a fundamentally crippled citizenry we exhibit a trait we shall examine in a separate chapter: rhetoricalness.

Curiously, the economic aspects of the land vary distinctly, according to the three periods in which we divide the course of our history. During the first, an unhurried period of consolidation, the distribution of land and Spanish territorial grants made the island a vast, half-cultivated farm with a considerable margin of undisturbed woodlands, pastures, marshes and inhospitable underbrush. In the second, restless and decisive, the land was fragmented into very ample plots where most interests benefitted more from the yield of small-crop farming, responsible for a major part of our diet. In the third, indefinite and problematic, the land loses its small landowner; the law limiting possession to 500 acres is disregarded; mass partitioning returns, but this time under a greater exploitation from absentee corporations that dietetically enslave our people by exercising a monopoly over the crops grown. Compare the imports of the nineteenth century to those of the twentieth century and the consequences of single-crop farming become apparent.

Only yesterday we took the land to heart and embraced it; today it is slipping out of our hands in a seesaw of sales, changing its patriotic value for an exclusively economic one. In the past when the land belonged to more than one and was at its best within the intervening arms formed by the landowner and the poet, it was not a cause for worry. Now that it belongs to private interests and has gotten itself into a predicament, it is not defined by the individual man but by the man within a syndicate. Yesterday Gautier Benítez, today the sugar mills. Notice in this particular case the course our lives will take, from the individual to the corporate. Mass production means an excess of two or three products but a lack of everything else.

The land then finds itself in this painful process of transaction, which is rather like saying historic-economic transition. What will become of the land? No one can say as long as the country that is to have the last word remains unknown.

A home is a flower on the land. The *bohío*, made of straw and *yagua* palm, is a decorative detail in the regional landscape so picturesque from a distance but so dismal up close. It is destined to disappear because it does not represent the permanent qualities of any tradition. Its absence need not be regretted since the *bohío* is nothing more than a symbol of penury and misery. If every *jíbaro* could have a comfortable and safe home, made out of cement or wood, with metal roofs, indoor plumbing and modern conveniences, so be it; it is all to the good that the *bohío* be relegated to a place in history, poetry and folklore.

Scenery does not warrant protection; what should be of concern is essence. Appearances are mere externals. The *bohío* can only be defended from a purely economic plane; it is preferable that our *jíbaro* own his rustic house than that he become a mere renter of a modern one. When the *jíbaro* can put his home on the same level as those we own in the city, no one should bemoan the exchange of his pigsty and the elimination of that picturesque note so destined to disappear from our landscape. I daresay the storage shed or storm shelter is more essential and necessary than a straw hut.

Furthermore, the indigenous *bohío* cannot be the main ingredient in our housing formula because it is unsafe and flimsy. Look to Spanish contributions that responded to the needs of colonial

Puerto Rico: brick or cement walls; roof or brick tile; tall, wide doors and large, louvered windows. Intense heat, earthquakes and hurricanes determined the course of our island architecture, which we have practically abandoned. The zinc and glass panes predominating in homes today are foreign features superimposed over old building blocks. But imitation hurts us and is inconvenient. The tropics demand an especially strong and durable construction, very much its own, to respond to buffeting from its three natural enemies: hurricanes, tremors and the destructive effects of saltpeter and moths.

Had we been able to continue developing our collective psyche without impediment, perhaps we would have a fully evolved regional architecture using adobe instead of zinc and glass, which are not produced here. By mastering that raw material, said architecture would be responsible at the same time for a flourishing native industry that has completely disappeared: tile and brick masonry.

Inevitably we will have to return to this. The climate, storms, national economy and necessity itself require the creation of housing that will respond effectively to the needs of the territorial temperament. The orientation of the land, and its significance, must be considered before availing ourselves of any other importation from the new culture that aids us today.

Pretension and Artistic Expression

Let us see now to what extent the people and their surroundings project themselves in the sensitive world of literary art. We are going to walk through an entangled field, foggy and off the beaten track, still uncharted by the critical adventures of explorers. Our wanderlust did not have the leisure necessary for artistic creation or the exploration of bedrocks that could serve the scholar as bases of support for creating an intellectual cartography. Lack of records, libraries and museums to guide the efforts of researchers with original works has been a formidable barrier to arranging and appraising our unplumbed literary production. If we discount two or three incomplete monographs yet to be published, and one or two published, clearly much remains to be done.

We lack a comprehensive work regarding the literature of Puerto Rico. To date no one has bothered to compile the list of our expressions. A collection of our songs and poems has not been done either. There remain countless untouched topics in the arsenal of our bibliography that require development. A small sampling from the large basket of topics that would have facilitated the pressing aspirations of this chapter include: printing in Puerto Rico, influences on our literature, native characteristics of same, development of our journalism, predominant ideas of the nineteenth and twentieth centuries, modernism and current aesthetic trends. We do not need a mariner's chart to set sail on the dead sea of the first three centuries of our history. There are no rocks, reefs, sand banks or difficult currents to make the traveler turn back in fear. Those centuries were blank pages in the history of our letters, with only three or four names so as not to be absolutely barren. Among them were García Troche and the canon Torres Vargas, historians who were forced by different official requirements to pen reports about the island, and Francisco de Ayerra y Santa María, Gongorist poet who lived in México but was born in San Juan in 1630. Any of them could be easily confused for the Spanish writers who during that first phase remained tied to our island: López de Haro, Bernardo de Valbuena, Juan de Castellanos and the most recent of all, Friar Iñigo Abbad.

These three centuries constitute an exasperating cultural desert in terms of artistic expression and coincide with the precarious course that our history took as the reader shall see further along. For us everything arrived behind the times and fell short of the original: the printing press, newspapers, book stores, libraries, institutions of higher learning, love of reading, prose for aesthetic purposes. In short, literature with all its conditioning elements is an art exclusive to the nineteenth century. We still had not started down the road of letters when Cuba could already count with several classics. Isolation and lack of initiative condemn us to receiving literary changes from the outside world with deplorable delay.

The printing press arrived in Puerto Rico in 1806. The first production of amusing literature on the island was not, as Menéndez y Pelayo affirms, the translation of *Anacreontics* and the classical myth of *Hero and Leander* or Graciliano Alfonso's *El beso de Abibina* (Abibina's Kiss), published in 1838. That distinction belongs to the works rarely signed that appeared in newspapers published between the birth of *La Gaceta Oficial* (The Official Gazette) in 1806 and *El Boletín Instructivo y Mercantil* (The Bulletin of Business Information) in 1839. Our beginnings are recorded in the columns of *Diario Económico* (The Financial

Daily) and *El Cigarrón* (The Cicada[7]), published in 1814, in *El Diario Liberal* (The Liberal Daily), published in 1821, and *El Eco* (The Echo) in 1822.

The first book of verse published in Puerto Rico, *El cuadernito de varias especies de coplas muy devotas* (The Booklet of Devotional Short Poems), was issued in 1812. It was published by a Capuchin missionary, Manuel María de Sanlúcar, "with only the pious end of encouraging devotion and promoting the divine praises that we owe the Lord of all creation." Later we find the name of an Iberian poet, Juan Rodríguez Calderón beside the song "A la hermosa y feliz isla de San Juan de Puerto Rico" (To the Beautiful and Happy Island of San Juan de Puerto Rico), and in 1832 the name María Bibian Benítez, our first native poet, whose "Ninfa de Puerto Rico" (Nymph of Puerto Rico) was included by Pedro Tomás de Córdoba in his then published *Memorias* (Memories). With the founding of *El Boletín* (The Bulletin), of impressive longevity, the terrain for anthologies is prepared.

As is apparent in the last two titles cited, Puerto Rico started to become a theme for poetic elaboration not as a definite reality, but rather a rhetorical formula that had not taken on any substance. Adjectives and persiflage tread one road; the social body they adorned tread another. Compare the poem by Juan Rodríguez Calderón with the great work of that other Spaniard, Jacinto Salas Quiroga, collaborator in *El Boletín* who insisted according to Tapia that, "Puerto Rico is the cadaver of a society that has not been born." We can say that in 1839 our incipient literary output still does not belong to us entirely. Our period of lactation is prolonged until the first half of the century ends.

In 1843 *El Aguinaldo Puertorriqueño* (Puerto Rican Christmas Carols), a collaborative work by natives and Spaniards, was published. Elated by this first communal statement, Puerto Rican students living in Barcelona converted their joy into *El Album Puertorriqueño* (The Album of Puerto Rico), published in 1844, in a show of support to what they called "a sign of life." In 1846 a

---

[7] A large winged insect, the male of which produces a shrill sound through membranes in the abdomen.

second edition of *El Aguinaldo Puertorriqueño* was published and in that same year the Barcelona contingent reciprocated with *El Cancionero de Borinquén* (The Songbook of Borinquén).

Despite being the bricks and mortar of our literary beginnings, these four books are still not a strong expression of our personality because they are ingenuously dominated by themes and standards already passé in Spanish literature. Their mimicry eclipsed any sign of originality; the babble of children was clearly heard. More was consumed than created. They were content to fill the simple demands of our markets, and since so little was solicited very little was given. Dilettantes of the colony had to band together to take their first walk in public. Only one stood apart from the rest, taking the lead with the first important book, a storehouse of our expression that moved us with its honesty and sense of patriotism.

To embark upon the subject that preoccupies us here it is necessary to gingerly reduce our list of literary saints to a few indispensable names, preferring those whose production approached the essential nature of this essay. This is due to the exigencies of space, the need to select, and because we refuse to make this book a congratulatory treatise.

After José Andino, the journalist, Manuel Alonso is the first author who in our estimation merits a place of distinction in our literary history for the quality and quantity of his work. When the first edition of *El Gíbaro* (The Peasant) appeared in 1849, our first literary star lit up the sky.

With Alonso, poetry, gone astray with foreign conventionalisms, found its very self. The land and the people did not have an effective place in our letters until this observer came forth prepared to sort out all our problems with grace and wit. He was the first writer to depict our everyday life and record our customs, and the first to pay critical attention to the work of a Puerto Rican poet. He also made our island a topic of preoccupation in the world of letters for the first time. With the appearance of Alonso the soul of Puerto Rico is found at long last.

More than a doctor of medicine (by specialization a psychiatrist) he was, by learning and sensibility, a pertinacious man of letters profoundly preoccupied with our rising national consciousness. His prose and verse throughout forty years, with few exceptions, addressed our pain. His was the first attempt, in *El Album*, at a poetic definition of the Puerto Rican prototype. He produced the first description of our customs in *El Cancionero*, and his was the brief yet most detailed record of this period and perhaps of all our literature in the nineteenth century, *El Gíbaro*. In it the most significant piece of our history is wonderfully summarized; the future will know of our traditions' infancy because of it, as well as our sorrows, beliefs, virtues, faults and the salient facets of our already centuries-old personality.

The juices of nationalism flowed from his innermost being, his discontent tempered by wit and usually hidden from the censors in amusing happenstance. In general his writings concealed deeper meanings. Just as there was more to a Puerto Rican than met the eye there was more to his work than met the eye. Lift the veil of witty remarks and before long you will see in his work the thorny nature of our situation and the only means we had then to safely expose it. At a more propitious time we will devote ourselves to his book with the thoroughness it deserves, pointing out the literary and the philological, in addition to its folkloric and ethnological value.

Distances notwithstanding, *El Gíbaro* is our *Poema del Cid* and our *Martín Fierro*. If by its form it tenaciously clings to Spanish literature, by its essence and feeling it pertains entirely to Puerto Rican culture. In his first poems Alonso could not elude the servile imitation that characterizes these literary beginnings. In *El Album* he wrote an imitation of *La Canción del Pirata* (The Pirate's Song) by Espronceda, which intended to treat the subject of *El Salvaje* (The Savage). And I say intended because Alonso hid nationalistic feelings in that unoffensive composition which otherwise could not be brought to the printed page. A sample of his prudent caution can be appreciated by the reader in the refrain:

It is my good fortune to live a free man
Without chains to oppress me;
Under their weight only slaves groan,
Not I.

From here one goes directly to the poem about "Agüeybana el Bravo" (The Fierce Agüeybana), written by the persecuted Daniel Rivera of whom we shall also speak in another chapter. His attempt at concealment was not entirely successful because the author received two admonitions in 1844: "one from his father," according to Salvador Brau, "in which the bad effect caused by the poem and suffered by the Count of Mirasol, General Captain of the Island, was brought to his attention, the other by D. Francisco Vasallo, meant to remind him of the conditions in the country for which he wrote his works." This thin-skinned reaction was an iron gag that stifled our best artists for years. A short time later, when *El Gíbaro* arrived in Puerto Rico, it should come as no surprise that it was labeled as suspicious and held by Customs. Nevertheless, as a result of the opportune intervention of the bishop, Gil Esteve, the book had better luck than *La Peregrinación de Bayoán* (The Pilgrimage of Bayoán), an innocuous novel by Hostos, confiscated later by the government. In the end Alonso's triumph was complete; Puerto Rican Creolism saved his first august book.

Thirty years of public pressure induced Alonso to publish a second edition of the book. In my opinion this is the first Puerto Rican work that deserves the honor of republication. Despite its middle-of-the-road style and forced sleights of hand, *El Gíbaro* is really a precious escape valve for our rising patriotism. Recently, German philosopher Count Keyserling stated a truism that we should use as the basis for a plan of action: "The shortest path to finding yourself circles the world."

Alonso, a beacon in the darkness, walked down that path. After graduating in Barcelona he returned to Puerto Rico. From there he went to Galicia to practice his profession. He moved from Galicia to Madrid, where he succeeded in becoming General Serrano's physician. As Serrano was being persecuted, Alonso

35

was exiled to Lisbon. Later he returned to Madrid and finally to Puerto Rico where in 1882 he reprinted his book, adding a second volume the following year. Let us emphasize this point so key to understanding the essence of being *criollo*, or Creole. Before our first book of substance was completed its author, a man of letters, science and travel, journeyed through all of Spain, vitally enriching the breadth of his vision. Here is a standard for works of this nature.

Salvador Brau, another standard bearer of Puerto Rican-ness, whose beautiful introduction to the new edition increases its value, presents it with the furtive wink, the cautious protest, a dagger's blow given with a smile: "the intimate history of a people, but a history in which the reticent pen of the author has counted beforehand on the imaginative collaboration of his readers...; the mild-mannered appearance the book projects covers a climate of censorship where truth and shrewdness are on a par."

Here is the painful *via crucis* in our literature. Alonso was harmless, discreet to the point of timidity because he knew he was closely spied upon. In 1862 censors refused to publish the allusive romance "Todo el mundo es Popayán" (All the World Is Popayán) in *El Almanaque Aguinaldo* (The Christmas Gift Almanac). Our regionalistic authors had to dedicate themselves to sleight of hand, expressive extravagance, and prudent allegories to inconspicuously convey their views. The rest cultivated common ground, "universal themes" of interest to no one, subordinating not only themes to those of Spanish literature but judgment and selection of topics as well.

With the prolific exceptions of Salvador Brau in the short story, El Caribe in poetry, Ramón Méndez Quiñones in theater and Manuel Zeno Gandía in the novel (authors who along with other distinguished writers such as Daubón, Matías González and Virgilio Dávila continued the tradition that Alonso started), the best plots of land in Puerto Rican literature were, generally speaking, cultivated in limbo. Another outstanding exception— not counting journalists or historians—must be made for the venerable figure 0Manuel Fernández Juncos, the most illustrious promoter of our *criollo* letters. More recent exceptions must also be made of Juliá Marín, Meléndez Muñoz and Lloréns Torres.

Alejandro Tapia, as prominent and prolific as he is, is an excellent example of what I am saying. His most important dramas and novels do not possess the flavor of the land or the people. Harassed by censors since his beginnings, Tapia had to protect his talent by setting his work in other locales. Among his minor works, a few timidly approach the confessional, but none is in the same category as the aforementioned.

Tapia, however, is the writer who secretly undertakes the profound task that we point out in Alonso's work in a book not destined to see the light of day. I refer to the only parallel to *El Gíbaro*, created by Tapia so that we might capture the very marrow of *criollo* life. *Mis Memorias* (Memoirs) was published a few short years ago. More than an autobiography, it is a rich explanation of significant practices and abuses that, due to their informal and commonplace nature, do not figure prominently in our history. *Mis Memorias* is a textbook on our old customs with edifying and coordinated descriptions, clear sociological investigation, and a veracity that revealed the patriotism of one whom as participant and witness of the facts was at the same time its faithful historian.

Unlike *El Gíbaro*, *Mis Memorias* has the advantage of direct quotes and is free of allegorical or periphrastic stiltedness. Those who track down our essence by following the perceptible footsteps we left behind cannot but exclaim upon arriving at the grove of *Mis Memorias*: "Our nation passed through here." The opposite occurs with the poetry of Gautier Benítez; it is such light fare it makes no imprint on the land at all.

Gautier is a superficial poet, sentimental, romantic, faint-hearted. His two favorite themes are love and country. His work is typically melancholic, bucolic, musical. Because of his simplicity Gautier does not offer, as a whole, any difficulty in defining his monochromatic art. He is the poet of love for women, for neighbor

and for country. He lived ever in love with his land and showed
how to love her as one loves a bride, fashioning his rough and harsh
clay with a selection of infectious, sweet words.

While an incurable illness destroyed Gautier's lungs, a technical diffidence reduced the assertive independence of his judgment.
Both conspired with the hostility of the environment to eat away at
the core of his creativity. Gautier's limitations notwithstanding, his
countrymen lovingly ordained him the poet laureate of Puerto Rico.

For Gautier the country was the ideal woman, cause and repository of our emotional impulses. Four lines of his poem "Impetus"
indicate his mind-set:

> You give life to the maiden
> who inspires my frenzy;
> I love her because of you
> I love you because of her.

A descendant of Spanish poet Gustavo Adolfo Bécquer,
Gautier's lyricism turned into nostalgia, viewing a Puerto Rico
reflected in a mirror of water, regarding her in "Ausencia" (Absence)
or "Regreso" (Return) "like the memory of a profound love," with
the feeling of being in love that prevents men from probing and get-
ting to the bottom of things. What is worth noting in Gautier is his
tenderness, the shyness with which he sang about the generic surface of our landscape. He did not delve behind the scenes into the
people or their customs, or the bleak insular life weaving the drama
of their lives. His eyes took in the countryside, the cordial planes of
the topography, but very rarely and with great difficulty did he
reach the very fiber of our being.

Balseiro hits the target with keen marksmanship when he
states: "Gautier looks at Nature and sees the landscape in a generic
way. There is no sense of authenticity in his descriptions, or specific
characterizations in those things cited by him...he did not know
how to capture the spirit of the landscape and reproduce it objectively in his poems. He did not have, as José Santos Chocano has,
for example, eyes sufficiently scrutinizing to marvel at the soul of
Nature." Were we to substitute the name of Puerto Rico for any

other torrid land, his descriptions would not suffer any alteration whatsoever.

From hereon our patriotic poetry will follow this ineffectual course. A new attitude, however, particularly exemplified by the work of El Caribe (José Gualberto Padilla), will disrupt it now and then. This attitude is defensive, polemical, radiates outward, is "against" or "in favor of," is a poetry of rage and despair, written with closed fist and nerves on edge. This poetry rejects the lamentations of Jeremiah and feeds itself with the vitality of Ecclesiastes. It aggressively gets to the bottom of things and succeeds in producing expressive inventions. When concrete depictions are humorously done, grafting the waggish spirit of *El Gíbaro* upon the social family tree of *Mis Memorias*, the result is a skillfully crafted product.

The posthumous work by El Caribe, *En el combate* (In Combat), proves what I am saying. His pseudonym is itself an attempt to clearly state his identification with the native character. Padilla beautifully represents our lyric energy, not so much for his valiant response in verse to Manuel del Palacio, or for his festive satires, but for his admirable "Canto a Puerto Rico" (Song to Puerto Rico), which he left unfinished. By temperament and education he was able to handle native ingredients better than Gautier Benítez. "Canto a Puerto Rico" is the first known attempt at synthesis in our literature; it is a shame that this manifestation of native expression remains frozen just at the moment it was about to soar.

As we have indicated previously, nineteenth-century writers could not respond freely to the issues of their time. Looking at the past, they saw nothing but a desolate void of three idle centuries, and before them a sterilizing surveillance that prevented them from studying native ways or elevating the temperature of our collective personality to a fever pitch. The native character, still in formation, could not provide a sense of time or place, and the oppressive political environment inhibited them from creating one. Although the bold efforts of a few recorded a handful of basic characteristics and differences for posterity in a list of autochthonous traits, the easiest position to take was one of servile imitation. Its widespread practice and long history depict us, in terms of literature, as a colony of

Spain's literary realm or an extension of her literature. Where, then, do we command respect beyond our shores? What feature of *criollo* originality has made a lasting impression upon normative European technique? What contributions with regard to acquisitions have we made?

Just as there was never an effective insurrection in our history, neither was there one in our letters. Language, culture and aesthetics followed the official course of the censors, and although the threat of coming under suspicion stemmed the flow of criolloism (or Creolism), we have been able to air a few covert tatters from deep in the closet of our soul. From these tatters and only from these should our emancipation someday proceed.

Clearly this will not be achieved with the hackneyed ideas now in vogue, those personal trivialities that hardly interest and do not capture the imagination. These mimicking poets lack the internal pulse, *criollo* but universal, charged with contagious resonances that could sublimely stir the hearts of the rest. Yet enthusiasm is limited for these artists who meekly create without breaking the barriers produced by cultural immaturity. The hesitant literary steps of old men and youngsters should never be confused with the surefooted poetry seasoned by the salts of a fully developed culture.

I believe we are just beginning to convalesce from a prolonged bout of poetic pneumonia, but movement forward can only be achieved at the cost of hard work. We can point to good poets today and in the past, exact in meter, beautiful in rhyme, proper and perfumed, who have the old enchantment of Viennese waltzes. They create verse about a well-heeled society wrapped in ethereal smoke, always ready to show off their powdered wigs during the most complicated rigadoon. These poets, cornerstones of a heroic ilk, are perfect for albums and diaries. However, despite their exquisite exactitude they hold on to antiquated ideas like old spinsters who cannot find marriageable suitors. Literary competitions are still held for themes from bygone days: love, faith, one's country.

A permanent guard must be posted at the gates of sensibility to interrupt the traffic of all affectations and forbid the entry of these unhealthy purveyors of rubbish. Artistic transfusions and bourgeois grafts from the same donor demonstrate a splendid capacity to reinvent the wheel and the persistence of derivative work by indistinguishable authors. No one is interested any longer in lonely hearts, the legendary sadness of twenty-year-olds, flat depictions of the landscape, dreadful acrostics and ragged *décimas jíbaras* (folk songs) more ponderous than several pachyderms.

The island's poetry certainly includes a good number of *vedettes* who still perform honorably on our stage. A new group of performers must be awaited to pick up poetic activity from where the others left off. I respect any attempt at innovation for the new possibilities it may contain. That thing that around town is referred to as *atalayismo*, in my opinion, has a profound experimental feel only frightened souls find irritating. If instead of jeering, we adopted an inquisitive attitude, *atalayismo* could be seen as a yearning for novelty of expression, or at the least a rebellious gesture of a few young men who cannot content themselves with the literary insolence of our grandfathers. The movement would bear greater fruit despite its lack of popularity, which it does not need in any case. Greater understanding—if we are capable—can stimulate the movement and its proponents to go forward. Before anything else, we need to respect ourselves intellectually. I admire Evaristo Ribera for his obstinate poetic vocation and because he is an admirable example of what an artistic conscience can do. In a recent, lengthy essay I have tried to make the significance of a great Puerto Rican innovator, Luis Lloréns Torres, very clear. I have not been sparing in admiration or plaudits for another leader in new approaches, Luis Palés Matos, a solitary figure in the Puerto Rican byways of Afro-Caribbean poetry. These three men express our collective personality, and through their efforts brighten the prospects for our literary art. These are dark days, but if it were a time of yuletide cheer we indeed would have at hand the myrrh, the incense and the gold to make an offering to the Christ Child.

There is some discussion these days regarding the rationale (and unreasonableness) for an Antillean expression that blends the spiritual movements of the Larger Antilles. It seems to me we must first ask ourselves: What is Cuba? What is the Dominican Republic?

*Insular*ismo

What is Puerto Rico? In order to indiscriminately use an overall tone, the individual tone of each island must first be defined; once the nuance and measure of each country is elucidated, look then for the expressive balance of the Antillean triangle. Anything attempted without this guiding principle will be detrimental to any unifying aspiration.

In the debate to which I now allude, two antagonistic ideas stand face to face as enemies: universality and criolloism. Those who defend the concept of art without frontiers, without national boundaries and with cosmopolitan appeal would deny Creole poetry even its very reason for being. Their refusal is well taken if by *criollo* poetry is understood those coarse and horrible *décimas jíbaras* that are composed in Puerto Rico with impunity. To cultivate Creolisms there must be frugality; launching all this nonsense into the world to the tune of *tiple* and *bordonúa* guitars is like writing a check without funds. They bounce but cannot circulate.

Yet no one, no matter how myopic, can deny the existence of German, English or Italian literature. And within the wide parameters of what is considered Hispanic, Spanish literature and its offshoot Hispanic American literature fall into distinct categories. By offshoot I refer to Mexican, Chilean, Argentinean or Uruguayan literature. Even within Spain's literature one can discern differences among regions: Catalonian, Galician, Andalusian. Why shouldn't Puerto Rican literature stand on its own as well? Perhaps we have no reason to coin our own expressions knowing as we do those from Spain, Argentina and Cuba? Or do we lack the cultural funds to do so?

The world is not found by heading outward, but inward to the heart. Yet we must also remember the quote I cited previously, the shortest route to finding one's very self circles the globe. The universal, that abstraction which by being so common does not dwell in any one place, cannot be inconsistent with the national. "When the firm expression of artistic intuition has been achieved," Pedro Henríquez Ureña says, "not only is the universal sense in it, but the essence of the spirit that possessed it as well, and the taste of the land from which it nourished itself." The Portuguese poet Guerra

Junqueiro adds "if a poet does not feel what is 'round about him, tangible and living, with greater force than what is distant and abstract, he may be anything else, but a poet he is not."

Though our evolution is yet to be completed, there are distinctive echoes in the raw material we are perusing that only the Creole who is thoroughly educated will be able to hear. Due to their encyclopedic ignorance, our army of mediocre verse writers cannot hear the chords, much less the echoes of our specific character. Be careful, then, with imitation. It is very difficult for someone who lacks cultural sensitivity to detect the sources of genuine criolloism.

There is no more nationalistic writer in all of contemporary Spanish literature than Unamuno. Knowledgeable in dead and living languages, there is nothing fundamental to European culture that is unknown to him. There are probably few who understand Hispanic American literature better than he. Though a poet, he is very knowledgeable in sciences, mathematics, history; though a writer of prose, he is very learned in poetry. His knowledge of botany and economics have guided his aesthetic eagerness to make Castile known. In his work, Unamuno offers the world the exact measure of what is Castilian. And this very *criollo* man, universally read and admired, in his book *Contra esto y aquello* (Against This and That), expresses ideas that here are pertinent: "I am one of the many Spaniards who upon picking up a work from the Americas want it to convey a taste of the land and the people from which it sprung, intense and genuine poetry, not literature wrapped in decadent, ridiculously affected words and in exotic fake flowers....I am most interested in works that are most from their country, the most pure, the most typical, the least translated and translatable. The more one is of his time and his country, the more he belongs to all the ages and all countries."

Far from all partisan contact, and as a result of extensive research, I am in favor of cultivating a Creole art superior to that of our Manuel Alonso. We must desist from the voluntary abandonment of what is ours in order to end the disdain and indifference with which the world regards us. Creolism needs ideas far removed from the hamlet originating on the open road over which no mayor of municipal poetry can travel. Scribblers of *jíbaro* expressions are obstacles if their work does not transcend their reach. I have read nothing so devastating as the diffidence of Félix Matos Bernier when he said in *Recuerdos Benditos* (Fond Memories), "I deem it sufficient for my ambitions that my verses are read in the beloved piece of earth where I was born." That is not Creolism; it is provincialism.

The epigraph Muñoz Rivera chose for his poem "Paréntesis," "Fortunate the man who has not seen rivers other than those of his homeland," is another demonstration of shortsightedness no one should take seriously. The contagion of our isolation must be avoided and make its ties to our solitariness plain. We too form part of what is called "the universe," and it is necessary to cultivate our letters from the inside out so that they may have open passage.

Our literature has yet to articulately touch upon our interesting indigenous life, the defining attitudes of the conquistadors, the essence of our formation, the bitter roots of our beginnings or even the disquieting instability of these days. The seeds of our nationalism have not flourished thematically. Since the beginning our hearts have followed other disciplines, the sources of their passion were other things. Without *Pueblito de antes* (Small Town of Yesteryear) by our own Virgilio Dávila, the Creolism of small town life would still be lost to us.

We must learn to be *criollo* without arrogance. We must act upon our expansive and meaningful traits, the cosmic not the limiting, looking attentively at our people from the depths of our soul, until our expression becomes one with the image we see. "In art," says Ortega y Gasset, "everyone has the right to express what he feels. Very well and good, provided that he commit himself to feel what he should."

This indeed is not work for a seller of costume jewelry. Those whose spiritual reach falls short or whose scope of knowledge is limited shall be content to produce trinkets and baubles. The fitting expression of our character can only be made by one who can count on a broad cultural range worthy of such an undertaking.

The Course of Our History

Weighing Anchor

These essays began with three very decisive moments in the evolution of our country: its genesis (slow, receptive and hesitant during the sixteenth, seventeenth and eighteenth centuries); its growth (nervous, formative and dramatic during the nineteenth century) and the transitional period (insecure, unsettled and unstable during the twentieth century). The previous essay presented the characters and the backdrop of this drama. Now it is necessary to expose the controlling strings above the historical stage. In our desire to grasp the culture of our nation, we must make the import of her history clear.

Puerto Rico becomes a geographical reality with the Renaissance. The Middle Ages left us to piece together our prehistory with the immediate remains of an unclear indigenous past we have surmised with great difficulty. Clearly we lack a renaissance and a middle ages since we cannot consider our nineteenth century but an awakening—a birth—of our collective consciousness that begins to form slowly and silently in the gestating years of the sixteenth, seventeenth and eighteenth centuries. Our renaissance, in effect, lay ahead of us.

It is after the explorations, during the first hundred years of the island's Christian acculturation in the sixteenth century, that peninsular importations and the structuring of our political life took place. However these did not hasten any noteworthy individualistic traits to distinguish us. What did occur was the mere transplantation of conditions that could not yet confer, because of their tentative experimental character, differentiating traits. Our ancestors had changed their patches of land, but neither the geography, climate, nor the mixing of peoples had been able to effect a visible transformation in so short a time.

Later, in response to the needs of the new territory, laws acknowledging a new gestating consciousness are made to suit these lands and legally aid its prompt development. Yet colonization encountered serious difficulties, not only due to frequent wars sustained by Carlos V and Felipe II in the sixteenth century, but regrettably for all the ones lost by their successors. In the seventeenth century, drained by confrontations with England, France, the Netherlands, Italy, Portugal and Catalonia, Spain ceased to be an international power of the first order and entered a period of open political decline, its industrial, agricultural and commercial splendor extinguished by these wars and other domestic problems. The total depletion of the public treasury was not as great as the society's bankrupt mores. In the second half of the seventeenth century the mighty Golden Age reached a critical point, and since its founding our new colony has had to bear the brunt of Spain's decadence.

The development of Hispanic culture in Puerto Rico found itself hampered by ferocious piracy infesting the Caribbean waters at the time; by unsuccessful foreign invasions that so often declared us to be French, Dutch or English; by hurricanes; by the diatribe of the colonizers beginning in Juan Ponce de Leon's time. Conditions, including tumultuous periods in Spain and one fraught with incidents in Puerto Rico as a result, were not propitious for the unencumbered development of the peaceful arts. Dejectedly carrying the unbearable weight of our historic lot, we scaled the steep hill of two formative centuries until we reached the doors of the third, as rife in disastrous wars as the previous centuries.

In the eighteenth century Spanish culture lost its internal compass. Imbued with French formulas, neoclassicism corraled and muzzled the conquered national consciousness, took refuge in the short farces of Ramón de la Cruz and the paintbrushes of Goya, unable to free itself from the pain of Bourbon cultural and political influence to which it was condemned for many years. The eighteenth century contained great obstacles to the spontaneous continuity of the Spaniard's creative genius and its stagnation arrested the development of our people. In this manner the first episodes of Puerto Rico's history came to a close, and it is now helpful to briefly highlight conditions during its more important periods.

These first three centuries of our history are characterized not by progress but by the most senseless exploitation. In 1788 the first history of the island, [*Historia geográfica, civil y natural de la isla de San Juan Bautista de Puerto Rico*] was published. Written by the Spanish priest Iñigo Abbad around 1780, the book distinguishes itself, among other reasons, for the author's wise recommendations for alleviating the colony's serious ills. We can derive from his book our first treatise on social therapeutics. If the country lived a rudimentary and ill-fated existence during the sixteenth century, how does it ever cope with the eighteenth century?

Iñigo Abbad devoted five interesting chapters (20 through 24) to examining the reality of the time in which he lived. The first chapter, on the government, reaches this conclusion: "Whatever the cause, the island is very far from being in the fortunate condition it could have been in under the administration of learned, patriotic governors." The second chapter, which studied the population, complains about its sparseness and proposes measures to increase it. The third chapter is devoted to agriculture, stating that "the country has not taken a first step in establishing its agriculture." The fourth chapter deals with commerce, and as the peninsular port was the only one open to us you will be able to judge its importance by this statement: "Puerto Rican commerce with Spain is nil." The fifth chapter, the last analyzing the state of affairs in Puerto Rico toward the end of the eighteenth century, discusses the public treasury and declares the island is quite "burdensome to the Crown," does not cover its costs and that the treasury, as all else, screams for reform. It is wellknown that our treasury had been financed since 1586 with money sent annually by the Mexican treasury. Funds for education were next to nothing. Friar Iñigo does not devote any chapter specifically to public education though he adheres to the alarming declarations made by Count O'Reilly who states in 1765 that there were only two schools in Puerto Rico. Though O'Reilly's statements are exaggerated, the state of education certainly was worse than that of government, agriculture, the treasury and commerce. It was practically worse than useless.

Let us rely on the testimony of an impartial traveler who in 1797 left us a picture of the colony he visited during a scientific expedition. We refer to the French botanist Pierre Ledru, whose memoirs were translated into Spanish by Julio L. Vizcarrondo. With regard to our capital, Spain's port in Puerto Rico and also the most advanced and flourishing city, he says: "...the traveler would seek in vain for factories or schools. The people exist in complete ignorance. A few women and friars teach the fundamentals of religion and grammar to a small number of children; seven-tenths of the population cannot read." Seventy-six years later Vizcarrondo remarks that fortunately this picture, as sad as it was true, had changed favorably. A difference had been made in seventy-six years.

The conscientiousness with which Pierre Ledru writes is unequivocal when discussing politics and governance. A scientist to the end, he wants to be fair, honest, exact. He points out the difficulties he had writing this chapter in an explanatory note that is valuable for us: "Public administration in Puerto Rico is enveloped in such shadow and mystery that a foreigner can hardly penetrate them."

For the *criollo*, neglected and disregarded by the peninsular organization of the State, its shadow government grew along with its fabled mystery. Once the colonizers became aware of México and Peru's extra riches, the Creole population faced a disheartening existence without regulatory participation in official government activities, and with no political rights or socioeconomic incentives. To our untold detriment, the center of attraction in the New World changed. Emigrations started to drain the country and the central government diverted its attention elsewhere. Printing was established in México in the first half of the sixteenth century; Puerto

Rico had to wait until the beginning of the nineteenth. Immediately thereafter the universities of México and Lima were founded; ours dates back to 1903. Why continue? We already know the devastating portrait painted by Friar Iñigo Abbad.

In 1799, after 300 hundred years of colonial life, Puerto Rico had little more that 153,000 inhabitants spread throughout thirty-four settlements. A century later in 1899 the country was able to double the number of towns and more than sextuple the population. The enormous difference between the first period and the second is too obvious to comment on; it is the same that exists between an illiterate people, lifeless, colorless and paralyzed, and another who is mindful of itself and zealously preoccupied with its potential.

Whosoever wishes to know fully the enormous difference between the first and second period of our history must refer to the splendid notes to Iñigo Abbad's historical account written by José Julián Acosta in 1866 and which complement it up to that point. One can see the difference in the historiographic method: All the historical reports from colonization through Iñigo Abbad's work, including Tomás de Córdoba's, were written according to official criteria responding, for the most part, to questionnaires submitted by the Spanish government. Officials did not consider the causes and consequences of the facts, or analyze and interpret with impartiality the detailed events. A methodical approach to history, with scrupulous documentation and of a scientific nature, begins with Acosta and is improved upon by Brau during the period in which Puerto Rican culture begins to mature.

In this period subconscious forces in our people began to dart forward, their lethargy not as profound and prolonged as in prior centuries. Contraband stealthily opened for us the international panorama, and as we defended our shores from foreign attack we prepared several talented minds—Campeche, Power and Andino—for the future. All were exceptions to the very patriarchal and vegetative rule of the eighteenth century.

"The son of the colonist," wrote Coll y Toste, "who learned to read and write correctly did so thanks to some roadside teacher or virtuous lady who dedicated herself to teaching. Education was looked upon with the greatest indifference and apathy, and no books of any kind were read. The islander had no individual or collective initiative and put his public life in the hands of higher government authorities. Political and administrative centralization, ingrained in the country since the first days of colonization, conditioned them to this defective system."

So we see that the value of a person and his or her intellectual assets were as insignificant as the abundance of rural products. Open fields were reduced to a few sugar plantations and those operations in decline were usually carried out by dealers in leather, cotton and ginger. Life in Puerto Rico, still untamed, completely absorbed the attention of our men who did not have the leisure necessary for intellectual exchange. Curiosity, analysis, and a preoccupation with a common cause had not yet developed. Since the colony lacked a strong profile, national pride could not go about testing its mettle. Without having yet embarked upon their own life, our people appeared exhausted after 300 years of colonization when, in reality, they were not yet born.

If during the eighteenth century artistic production atrophied and languished in the Iberian peninsula, one need not entertain its idea in any way, shape or form in Puerto Rico. Literary art and printing were unknown. Fernando Callejo, our best musical historian, maintains that "musical art was entirely in diapers toward the end of the eighteenth century, its only manifestations in religious music...with no information indicating the form in which dance music was produced."

Let us not mince words. The eighteenth century continues to be a great blank in our historiography. The little substantial information we have at this time indicates that essentially nothing had changed in the slow and colorless gestation of the Puerto Rican psyche.

Looking for Safe Harbor

When a radical change took place in Spain's fate, historical repercussions indirectly affected and galvanized our people. At the start of the nineteenth century when Bourbon rule was at a critical point, an awakened national consciousness resisted the Napoleonic invasion, and in the Courts of Cádiz liberal concerns joined together, delineating a new political course of action that continues to this day, namely, the Spanish parliament. These strong upheavals in the mother country opened a crack in the flank of our isolated ship and through it escaped the first sound made by the Puerto Rican nation, the primal scream of our very being. Our awakening occurs with the peremptory instructions given in 1809 by the municipal government of San Germán to Ramón Power, first Puerto Rican deputy to the Courts. The directive initiated the demand for collective rights that Puerto Ricans since then, and to this day, have made.

"Puerto Rico in the first decade of the nineteenth century," writes Salvador Brau, "was not the boorish bunch described by O'Reilly in 1765. With the increase in professional employees and business communication, and the immigration of Frenchmen and Dominicans, new ideas and procedures favorable to the development of our culture were introduced." Ramón Power, who became vice-president of the Courts of Cádiz, started by obtaining the annulment of the so-called absolute powers of the governors, and other political reforms such as the creation of the Intendancy, a provincial office separate from the general government.

But where one most perfectly sees the impact of a gestating Puerto Rican consciousness is in Power's selection for administrator of the Intendancy, Alejandro Ramírez, a very learned and courageous man who came to Puerto Rico to assume the post. Public finances were in ruins. The famed money transfers issued from Cartagena for years, but coming primarily from México's coffers to make up for our treasury's inability to bear the island's burden alone, ceased as of 1810 with the revolutionary movements started in México by Hidalgo. Upon the arrival of Intendant Ramírez, government revenues yielded 70,000 *pesos*; merely one year later, after establishing serious economic reforms and opening new ports to commerce, the public treasury collected close to 243,000 *pesos* in duties alone. In addition, the founder of Puerto Rico's Treasury Department generated new sources of income; reorganized the old ones; founded the *Diario Económico de Puerto Rico*; and established the Economic Society of Friends of the Country which quickly, and until 1898, became the most steadfast force in promoting the island's culture.

Ramón Power died in Cádiz. José María Quiñones (from San Germán) moved to Spain to replace him, only to see the despot Ferdinand VII trample over the Constitution and dissolve the Courts in 1814. Intendant Ramírez managed to obtain the *Cédula de Gracias* (royal decree of reforms) from the monarch, by virtue of which direct commerce abroad was established and foreigners from friendly nations were admitted, as well as other beneficial privileges. In 1816 this great benefactor upon whom the national conscience had buttressed itself departs, having opened the country's doors to numerous Venezuelan immigrants who breathed new life into our developing culture. To be sure, the names of Ramón Power and Alejandro Ramírez must be etched in stone for their early contribution to securing our collective identity.[8]

Our new circumstances met with a series of obstacles from Spain, including Ferdinand VII's absolutism and Alfonso XII's

[8] What Ramírez was to the Treasury, Father Rufo was to Education twenty years later.

54

restoration to the throne. The discoverer nation had to shift all its attention to resolving domestic problems and civil disputes. Forgetting about colonial problems, Spain naturally turned a deaf ear to overseas protests because Carlista wars, constitutional issues, frequent military insurrections, changes in government—monarchical, provisional (1868), republican (1873)—religious strife and the Moroccan war were demanding all her attention.

Nevertheless, throughout this intricate web of historical mishaps, the barely visible threads of our nascent personality were turning into yarn. That embryonic idea which takes demonstrative shape through Ramón Power in 1809 was filling our collective mind with aspirations, demands, disappointment and fulfillment, and making ever more clear and precise our makeup as a new people. The initial mandate commissioned to Power went through a series of changes in its evolution that introduced the free press; diverse popular movements; the beginnings of native literature; the abolition of slavery; Court reports; the development of public education; the emergence of political parties; an awareness of the obligation to be Puerto Rican first and foremost; and the foundation of our own athenaeum (*Ateneo*). Ultimately the mandate developed into the ephemeral autonomy granted by Spain in 1897. Each push of our gestating consciousness gave rise to persecution, imprisonment, banishment, censorship of the press, abuse and repression that aided, more than deterred, our painful birth.

The most important event in this second period is the breaking of tactical Spanish policy in the nineteenth century. Puerto Rican opinion, with premeditation and caution, stands up to Spanish opinion. The *criollo* position responded to an inner force more than to exterior pressures. This victory for the island's point of view has its best official supports in native-born representatives who begin to occupy posts in town councils. One thing is certain: We were not able to rise from municipal government to executive government, but from these town councils we began to weigh the chances of officially advancing our own agenda, gradually creating camaraderie on the tropical island.

Since then political abuses, excessive taxes, exorbitant tariffs, credit restraints, domination by political bosses, usuries, privileges for some and ill treatment for others could no longer be carried out with support from our abetting silence. We met these difficulties with protestations, claiming as our due equal political status with the Spanish citizen. We demanded reforms and representation of our local interests "without distinction or disallowance of any kind" to avoid the "governance by entities hundreds of miles away and unfamiliar with local needs." We objected to the idea of assimilation by raising the liberal idea of autonomy, and our best men endeavored to bridge the distance existing between loyalty and servility, so often considered synonymous.

The native-born Puerto Rican never renounced the Spanish part of his identity, but he always considered himself a Spaniard "from here" with opinions and attitudes distinct from those "over there." The handful of separatists never constituted a sizable group; the liberals, reformists, abolitionists and nationalists, that is, autonomists, were legion. Sometimes they were unfair to Spain due to the disrepute in which her governance of the island often fell. Despite the fact that the discoverer nation was under the moral obligation to support its governors, differences could always be noted between the government there and the government here. Spain was one thing, its governors quite another. To emancipate our society we had to confront both many times. We could endure being a colony better than we could endure being a prisoner.

Thus we begin to work out our spiritual differentiation[9] in the nineteenth century, openly declaring it and operating within the already advancing biological differentiation of the previous centuries. Just when we succeeded in taking the reins of our collective destiny in our own hands, the Spanish American War vitiated our attempt, leaving us half formed and with the problematic drawbacks of beginning to be something else.

In the twentieth century a new ideological order changes the course of our nascent personality and our culture enters the period of transition in which we still live.

9 We refer the reader to a later chapter, "Puerto Rican Affirmation," which complements this one and dicusses what was omitted here.

Intermezzo: A Ship Adrift

In the twentieth century the needle of our people's compass changed northward, leading the way to a transformation that to date is more external than internal, but that little by little is tempering our interior lives. Let us step back a bit from the major events of our history and look for signs at the margins of current events that better define this period.

The year 1898 found us establishing a semblance of autonomy in our country under a charter we hardly had a chance to implement. Just as we were about to embark upon a new political life, the Spanish American War spoiled our chances, and our proper development suffered a setback. When President McKinley checkmated the king of Spain we unsuspectingly passed from a state of European polarization into a state of North American polarization. Ever since then the pieces on the Puerto Rican chess board have been moving in other directions.

Our psyche feels itself moving like a pendulum, migrating between two ways of life, releasing and absorbing, coming and going, a bird in flight restlessly seeking its course. Our country was in a tough period of transition, sandwiched between two antithetical cultures. We went from a Catholic State, traditional and monarchical, to one that is Protestant, progressive and democratic, from the cultured to the civilized, from the sociologist to an economist.

Any Puerto Rican whose vision has not been blurred by antagonism or idolatry can see the wonderful progress achieved in the last thirty years. Industry, commerce, agriculture and public wealth have all expanded tremendously; we have learned business techniques and the secrets of the economy. The new civilization has undeniably and promisingly transformed our existence as we can also act with greater freedom and protections now than during any other period. The change has taken us by surprise, and progress is widely acknowledged. We certainly have more schools and more roads than before.

We must remind the reader that the problem we raise here is not one of civilization but of culture. The fact that both terms may fruitfully interact does not mean they should be confused. If what we said in the first of these essays is heeded, the disassociation between both terms, authoritatively sanctioned by a series of illustrious thinkers starting with Jean-Jacques Rousseau and ending with José Ortega y Gasset, is distinctly understood. Culture implies more than progress. It is a vital force and must not be confused with civilization. It is more a qualitative than a quantitative matter. Facts and figures, the emblems of our time, cannot grasp it completely.

Our present culture frequently assesses itself by considering economic progress, sanitary conditions, roadways, and the volume of exports and imports, as though technical advances and North American mechanization were the barometers apropos for measuring the sensibilities of a people shaped by another value system. There are many writers who draw comparisons, applying pluses and minuses to contemporary life as if the territorial spirit could be reduced to statistics. The greater number, the larger amount, the official data, these serve as the standard upon which to compare the past with the present.

Enthusiasm for comparisons permits a reasonable man like Dr. Juan B. Soto to assess our current circumstances, saying in 1926 that "the progress achieved in Puerto Rico in the last twenty-seven years has no precedents in the economic history of humanity." Later on he states that our "society...and capabilities...can be favorably compared with the societies of some of the most highly civilized countries in the world." All this despite what the comparers fail to mention: If it is true that we have more schools and more sugar mills, more trades and more of everything, it is no less true that we have also had an inordinate increase in the number of bankruptcies, suicides, lunatics, criminals, TB cases, fraud, unskilled laborers and poor wretches in general. The population increase does not explain the corresponding level of collective misfortune we have reached.

Justifiably, those who compare will say that today schooling is available to the masses and therefore the illiteracy rate has decreased sharply. Public education, like nearly everything else in contemporary life, has unquestionably developed on a grand scale. But the most profound dimension of our culture does not pertain to length or width but to volume. Civilization is horizontal; culture vertical. If I were to join the group that defines everything in terms of pluses and minuses, I would say that today we are more civilized, but yesterday we were more cultured.

There is no point in marveling at the number of professionals we have today when there are cultured men who hardly know how to read and write, and very uncultured professionals who live comfortably from their profession. It seems that the ideal of education these days is none other than preparing a man to provide for his daily needs. This preoccupation with material things is shameful in view of José la Luz Caballero's beautiful axiom: "To educate is not to prepare a man for a profession, but to temper his soul for life." It is well and good that we take an interest in the making of citizens but it is wrong to neglect the making of men. *Une tête bien faite* is in every respect preferable to *une tête bien remplie.*

Our educators have not been able to freely develop an educational philosophy that will direct our youth toward fixed objectives. Where are we going? What should the definitive status of the island be? Federal state? Sovereign republic? Autonomy under a protectorate? In that hotbed of uncertainty called legal terminology, we presently belong to, but do not form part of, the United States. Without the assurance of a stable political future, schools have not been able to send forth citizens with a straightforward sense of direction.

The unsettled issue of bilingualism clearly demonstrates the instability of the historical moment we are now living. The necessity and obligation of managing both languages to perfection is indisputable. It would even be useful to learn French, German and Italian. I do not believe learning English has marred in any fundamental way the purity of the Spanish language. The deterioration it suffers in rigor is more than compensated by the great care and devotion with which it is studied today. On the other hand, teaching all assignments in English decreases the use of Spanish and there are moments in which we even lack the vocabulary to express ourselves in simple, basic conversations.

In my view the problem is more quantity than quality. The mother tongue is degenerating into nasal stammering, and the consequences of the language's impoverishment will prove fatal for our culture in the future. Despite the official status of English, the vernacular tongue still has the advantage at the present time. We must avoid being suspended between the two at all costs, not on the basis of attacking English in the name of purity, but on the basis of defending Spanish in the name of vocabulary. One need not heed the patriotic drivel that disregards the reality of consummated deeds in 1898 and passionately attacks the teaching of English, as if that instruction were not a means of enfranchisement for our people.

If the official language has not fundamentally altered—at least till now—the purity of the Spanish language, it does nevertheless make learning a torturous and discouraging process for the student. The mysterious leavening with which the vernacular language daily nourishes a child's spirit is not fulfilling its mission. Our mother tongue cannot induce higher aspirations in youngsters because during the time when it is propitious to do so, English imposes itself throughout the disciplines. This is how we slowly lose the most expressive dimension of our culture, its erudition.

To avoid this, English should be taught as an optional course, as is done in other places where there is no bias toward it. Along with Epifanio Fernández Vanga, I believe that "a child who lives with two languages never becomes 'twice' the man, but always remains 'half' a man." A thing half formed, no matter how civilized it may be, cannot serve as a model for the highest expression of a people.

Since we did not have the opportunity to train ourselves in the affairs of state during the last century, when the sovereign changed we fell flat on our faces before a democracy, and so we have inevitably helped to create a mediocrity. Bourget states that democracy will lose in depth what it gains by extension. It is true; the [United States is the] empire of the number and the middlebrow. It inadvertently excludes the exceptional collaboration of the best. With equal opportunity for all, the common man has felt satisfied to see his values elevated at the expense of a decline in the values of cultured men. Today cunning and audacity are attributes considered more useful than merit, dignity or principles. It is saddening to see the superior men and women of our country retiring to the isolation of their homes, burrowed to protect their dedication to excellence from the disrespectful domain of mediocrity. Unfortunately their protective isolation deprives our society of the very models it needs.

Democracy, in crisis in most of the world today, has established standards to benefit the incompetent and begrudges any favoritism to the intelligent. At one time we were told the best men for the best jobs. It turned out that the best men were found in mediocrity. Democratization of public education provides for the majority without proportionally supporting minorities who find themselves forced to lower their standards.

According to the Puerto Rican educator Pedro A. Cebollero, "this pseudodemocratic notion of distributing culture the way an inheritance is distributed, that is, equally among the heirs, is the result of an enormous absurdity since the ability to acquire culture does not correspond to the ability to acquire property, but varies from person to person." The same occurs in public life. If Ortega y Gasset were Puerto Rican, he would have written his book, *La rebelión de las masas* (The Revolt of the Masses), twenty-five years ago. This equalizing of human values brings with it a confusion and disorder that our poet Luis Palés Matos marvelously summed up in a painful phrase, *"Puerto Rico: burundanga"* (Puerto Rico: hodgepodge, an unholy mess of disconnected elements of questionable value).

Besides reinforced concrete, ready-made clothes and canned foods, three basic attitudes have been incorporated in our lives during this last period: an economic interpretation of life, a greater participation in civic matters and a fondness for sports. The first is responsible for measuring everything in terms of pluses and minuses, as if each thing and every attitude had a price in American gold. The second becomes booty coveted by all political parties and produces a pathological eagerness for government employment. And the third sounds a note of cheer in our sad night, developing wholesome, happy and feisty youngsters. Of these three attitudes, the economic is the most imperious and reckless.

We must acknowledge that the United States is a progressive, organized and technical nation. Its young, athletic constitution is a tribute to modernity. Compared to slow and conservative Spain, it proves to be much faster and up to the minute. Whatever is current is generally of a transitory nature. In Spain the act of conserving is implicitly an attempt at eternity.

Things from Spain age better because they are made for more than just the moment. More time and skill is employed in making them so they are difficult to destroy when style and progress want to replace them with new models. A Spanish chimney, house, wall or road is a paean to indestructibility. What a marvel to behold the colossal strength of old brick bridges constructed in an era when the invention of enormous trucks that today cross over them was not even suspected! Old buildings challenging time, cyclones and earthquakes continue to offer splendid service to countless offices of the insular and federal government.

In this day and age, we no longer have the leisure necessary for creativity because someone told us that time is money; yet the amount of money we lose is so much! We are always in an electric hurry to do things and though these things in fact end up poorly done, what we seem to care about is that they be up to date and done quickly. I have come to believe that the only motive for public works construction is justifying their inaugural festivities. Periodically the island proffers cyclones a steady diet of rural schools, and bridges are constructed only to see them floating upon rising rivers. On the domestic front, compare the admirable durability of old furniture with the ephemeral life of current pieces, and one will appreciate the change the very concept of time has undergone among us.

The difference that exists between the *danza*, tenuous and slow, and the quick fox-trot is the same existing between the life of yesteryear and that of today. Rampant materialism does not leave time for discussing meaty topics on culture, and if there were audacious men who dared do so, there would be no dearth of those considering so fine a spiritual act a waste of time. Thousands adhere to the dismal excuse of having no time to read, and the art of pure conversation has been deteriorating for years. We have suffered a deplorable decline in social calls, gatherings and club meetings. Our famous craft centers, exquisite oasis of noble workers, are disappearing appreciably.

If time is money, let us say of our own account that haste tramples a man's spirit; it is a poison. Socializing itself is in crisis because we lack the free time it requires. In official circles there is too much talk. In barbershops and drugstores, secrets and private lives are discussed openly. These days lucid, discreet conversation does not have as many practitioners as gossip. To cultivate the former some legislator should promote hygienic measures to regulate the prattle. If there truly is little time for anything, let us subtract that which is spent on bad habits in order to cultivate old virtues.

What happens with time also happens with its counterpart, space. Today, impressive communication systems have shrunken the distances between towns. Our island seems to have become smaller. Old ancestral mansions, as large as warehouses, have given way to compact housing, constructed tightly to economize on costly space. As everything is scrupulously measured—and charged for—we have learned to erect a few floors above each other, or in its absence to be crowded together in unsanitary conditions in an uncomfortable set of rooms. The agglomerating of the census, piling 485 inhabitants in each square mile, diminished the land's dietary support we once had at our disposal. We do not fit in our own homes and this discomfort painfully infringes upon that margin of happiness to which all people are entitled.

Educational specialization also reduces the spiritual space in which an individual moves. A man who has not made the reasonable sacrifice of acquainting himself with areas foreign to his specialization during his professional preparation will not understand, as is his duty, the difficulties overcome by others. We must violently break out of the prison of our professions and trades, to enlarge our mental and emotional space and free the soul from its confinement.

If we do not want to increase the ignorance of the so-called cultured class, other interests beside our own must be considered. Life's landscape should not be traversed with blinders on, under penalty of increasing the genuine predicament of our country. One can be a mechanic or a teacher, a doctor or a businessman, without becoming disaffected with cultural matters.

To those drawing comparisons, bear in mind that it is impossible to get to the bottom of our collective psyche in a crude vehicle of pluses and minuses. The objective purpose of statistics—a soulless method and science without a conscience—only captures the surface of an entire reality. It is incapable of penetrating the kingdom of a soul in purgatory. Statistics are a calumny with which science takes revenge on the soul. All peoples have a repertoire of inexplicable convictions, active and hard to grasp, that cannot be reduced to numbers. It is not possible to incarcerate men in the uncomfortable cage of a standard, a fetish that democracy has invented to avoid the complications commonly generated by differences.

Disastrous enthusiasm for the economical and utilitarian cuts useful items from the insular and municipal budget when these do not produce tangible profits. Official lack of concern for the finer aspects of culture, an indifference neutralizing worthwhile initiatives, has made itself felt in the country since the invasion began. "One of the first acts of the North American government in Puerto Rico," says Fernando Callejo, "was the elimination of all subsidies of an artistic nature." The current government is not interested in literature or music, painting or any other thing in which aesthetic pleasure plays a role.

A Ministry of Fine Arts would be highly unusual in the current administration. The government cannot afford this kind of luxury. There isn't even a bad museum, an academy of music or an official painting competition. There is no generous support for the *Ateneo*, no interest in popular arts or any meaningful expressive activity that in the past century had been lovingly supported through exhibitions, fairs, public competitions and government interest.

Municipalities demonstrating a love for reading in their budgets are extremely rare. Making them understand that a town library is as important as a marketplace or a slaughterhouse is an uphill battle. Town life is intellectually bankrupt. Years ago many towns maintained an excellent social life that alternately included concerts, soirées, open-air concerts, town festivals honoring patron saints, amateur societies, home gatherings devoted to conversation and religious formalities. Humacao, Guayama, Juana Díaz and San Germán, so deeply affected by the former culture, are today mere municipalities. Mayagüez, once a center for cultural events, today is a factory town. Only Ponce falteringly resists the destructive contamination.

Today all festivities, dances or dinner parties include liquor. We artificially dull the senses to more fully enjoy ourselves. Intangible enjoyments have become an awful bore unless alcoholic diversions are involved. What is more, amusement has become big business; everything must be paid for. Even horse races, so loved by old Puerto Rican racing enthusiasts, became a money-making spectacle the same as boxing. Wherever we attempt to flee, materialism is always one step ahead of us.

As the matter stands, two ways of life, at bottom quite different, find themselves at odds. Let us not ascribe to either one the universal conditions that have prevailed in each era. Many changes in our country that are attributed to North Americans do not exactly issue from them, but from the era that imposes them equally in Australia, Spain, Chile and Puerto Rico. Beneficial change, from wherever it may come, is inevitable and necessary. All peoples who want to keep their lungs healthy must breathe fresh air from the outdoors.

Though our identity sails adrift at this stage, it is not shipwrecked as some pessimists believe. All was never joy and jubilation; today, all is not misery and despair. We enter the twentieth century with a handful of useless remnants and a good number of social needs that we are gradually correcting thanks to the change of sovereign. At the same time, however, our life falls apart within a sordid utilitarianism, and culture has lost its finest impulses because of the plebeian intellectual pauperizing to which present-day vulgarity has subjected it. Radical change is responsible for the instability that bewilders us today. The duality within which our people move is the best indication of their erratic state.

When considering the tumultuous circumstances of the moment, I have often thought that today's moral physiognomy consists of transitory, provisional features. We become formed and deformed at the same time, winning and losing with each metamorphosis. Transformation generally implies a drastic alteration in habits and customs, and generates plaguing doubts about the very precepts of life.

I conclude by calling attention to our need to get a firm and clear handle on the central events that make up the skeleton of our moral frame and structure. Because of the nature of our people, the shortest path to fostering the purest ethics is the aesthetic one. In these hours of acute crisis for our culture, we must cultivate self-confidence, and concern ourselves with producing exceptional citizens. The allures of public life must be changed and the meaning of politics broadened until its repugnant irregularities are completely cast aside. We must demand that the press fulfill its mission to inform the public, universities maintain high levels of scholarship, and people sacrifice and give unselfishly. Strength of character, self-sufficiency, understanding, temperate stimulation, coordination of goals—here are the fields that need to be seeded.

Since we are in the process of mutation we must take care not to lose our resolve. Apathy at a critical moment like this, in addition to being reprehensible, is devastating. If during this crisis in our culture we marshal efforts to cultivate one common hope; if we wipe the corridors of public life clean of hollow men, worn by discord and ill will; if we remove the encumbrance of so many uncultured professionals masquerading as superior men when they are no more than newsmongers, quacks, ambulance chasers, schoolmasters, sacristans or alchemists; if, finally, we attend to the incubation of our collective soul, watching out for the transformation of the caterpillar until its pupal skin is shed and relatively independent movement is ensured, then I am certain that in the not-too-distant future we shall see a butterfly take flight.

*Insular*ismo

Past and
Present
Faults

Chess Table

There are a multitude of distasteful and pervasive cultural problems we should not gloss over, but for the purposes of this essay their discussion must be kept to a minimum. The norm has been to approach these problems from an emotional and patriotic point of view, sliding down the slippery slope of explanatory expediency. Such attitudes can be dangerous and useless: dangerous because prejudiced eyes view matters while clinging to partisan ideals, useless because study and reform that do not answer to the plain unadulterated truth are ineffectual in correcting problems. Applying solutions that do not address the total picture may cause dire consequences. Once again we stumble upon a rhetoricalness that restrains, inhibiting us from grasping calmly and impartially what ails us.

We continuously hear the furious outcry against land monopoly by foreign corporations, absentee ownership, large country estates, duty tariffs, etc. We cast prudence aside in a sentimentally slanted explosion when we weigh these problems from an anguished contemporariness without taking into account the past or the future. In addition, the tendency has been to evade fundamental aspects that have repercussions on other problems with which they are intimately connected, tied, and fused in a complex whole. These intricate entanglements are usually evaluated by outside experts who arrive at lamebrain conclusions because they are not grounded in the national character. Remedies for alleviating our violent headaches have been numerous and unsuccessful. Experts thought the malady cured with the emollient salve of statistics. Natives thought the honey of patriotic sentiment was the answer. The eye and the soul must concur in order to arrive at valid conclusions. By the same token, study our problems from the inside out. Otherwise, we are in danger of resolving them by creating others.

Before we consider just how ill prepared we are today without mincing words, the circumstances extenuating our collective culpability must be kept in mind to be fair. The colonial period habituated us to solutions and remedies in which we have not had a say. Since colonial times our economic, social, military and religious problems have been completely and astutely resolved for us, without ever having us wrinkle our collective brow in our own self-interest. On various occasions we have changed our currency overnight and our Treasury. Divorce laws were instituted; church and state were separated. One army was traded for another and even our Constitution was changed without the slightest participation on our part. Today we lack that instrumental preparation all nations of the world bought with their blood and tears. Our civil war has always been between political parties led by the country's fathers who rarely extended themselves beyond their role as foster parents.

Without scars from experiences in other skirmishes, we face today's problems unburdened by the weight of sound judgment, but full of preconceived notions. We lack aplomb because we need a historical ego. We need that subconscious collaboration brought about by a culture forged from pain and sacrifice. "True values," Marañón said, "are communally arrived at through effort. They are in a hidden tabernacle that only opens before a sacrifice."

I believe this explains the lack of continuity in which our government scrambles. It looks ahead, toward an immediate future, without a long-term vision or perspective on the past. It shrinks from the deed, sheltering itself in the gesture. Speech making opens the floodgates for hundreds of educational proposals during every legislative period, none of which ever become law.

This lack of continuity and vision is clearly understood when we consider how our political parties have had to closely follow the movements of Spanish parties in the past, and North American parties today. This obligatory attentiveness was involuntary, a function of necessity, of being in step with the winning parties in those cities. This being the case, Puerto Rican political parties have had to go about changing their names, programs and even their platforms according to needs foreign to their own, sacrificing the true direction the common good should have dictated. In over four centuries of history our country has never produced a governor elected by the people. Its fate remains symbolized on our crest's Paschal Lamb, which instead of stating *Joannes est nomen ejus* could more accurately state the biblical proclamation "here lies the lamb to be sacrificed."

Due to a historical and ironic twist of fate, the most peaceful people in the world were governed under the Laws of the Indias by a Captain General since the landing of Columbus, and since 1898 by the War Department in Washington, D.C. A nation who never formed an army of any kind has always been in the hands of a military government. How can a culture that has never succeeded in resolving its own juridical misgivings grow into a strong and unique State of its own? Moreover, since we have been perpetually placed in hands never exclusively our own, we have not taken part in the organization of the higher body politic or experienced the sacrifices necessary and indispensable for creating national symbols like an anthem or a flag.

A country without an epic, without sweeping heroic gestures, without significant historical demonstrations, we have consecrated a crude, bucolic *danza* as our anthem, which despite this fact moves our very soul. With regard to a flag, we cannot come to an agreement, some preferring the cross, others the star. Even our coat of arms, graciously given to the island by the Catholic kings of Spain, has caused disagreements. At times the lamb is painted standing upon a rock; at others, it lies stiffly over a book (the correct version). In 1902 the insular government committed the error (later corrected) of changing the old coat of arms for a preposterous herald, a type of police shield on which appeared a boat balanced on an unbelievable string of sausages. The history of these symbolic vicissitudes is recorded by Mario Brau in his tract *Nuestro Blasón* (Our Heraldry).

The tragedy of governance begins with Spanish colonists in charge of the indigenous population, and the first governor, Juan Ponce de León, who prompted the first schism. Later the struggle continues between the clergy and the State, and afterward the captain generals whose personal ambitions knew no bounds. The Captain Generalcy was severed from the Intendancy in 1811 initiating the ill will between intendants and deputies competing for power. The clergy completed this triangle. In 1821 civil and military authority are ostensibly almost separated. At that time the intendant, Luis de Santiago, attested to the appalling way some of the mayors scribbled their names. Today, the official status of illiteracy has not changed significantly; the percentage is very large notwithstanding the census' exclusion of mayors, doctor and lawyers.

In the second half of the nineteenth century there emerged a handful of men of character who embodied a native political patriotism, as well as those astonishing long-lived *caciques* masked as patriots. The courageous Autonomist party, founded in 1887, is divided into factions in 1896. Since then the evolution of our parties is characterized by a coming together and a splitting apart of these factions, bound by the not-always-noble aspiration of obtaining a majority; elections tend to convert politicians into simple harvesters of votes. Men here move inescapably within an order arranged elsewhere, their lives as citizens essentially preordained, unable to make political decisions of their own free will. The civic will has suffered the fortunes of perpetual minorities who, in the manner of these minorities, lose in initiative what they gain in indifference. The greatest fault of our insular government is its lack of authenticity. Natural stream of consciousness genuinely flows if the consciousness is captain of its own destiny.

This obligatory inhibition impeded the course of said internal process, and so, with the change in sovereign, we tripped over democracy like startled little children. One can see the people's misconceptions as they convert public officials into bosses when in reality they are no more than public servants. The people still do not clearly understand the significance and duty of their representatives, and their obligation to support them only if their performance coincides with the will of the people.

Just observe the fear and sullenness with which the people visit a government office. They request information or defend their rights timidly as if they were prisoners on death row. Respect is all well and good, discretion and even patience, but not the groveling attitude, the slow hesitation of the enslaved, or the trembling supplications of those about to be executed. Seeing the haughtiness of some and the timidity of others, I've come to think when going to the polls that there are far too many electoral votes already null and void before they're cast.

Ignorance regarding the basic fundamentals of citizenship kept us from not only obtaining our rights by entreaty, but also from doing our duty. The greatest difficulty appears to be assuming our basic responsibilities in the democratic process and honoring without bargaining our share of obligations. "The nation," said Hostos, "imposes as many obligations as rights upon us; and if we do not know how to perform these duties how can we complain about not enjoying the rights?" The person who can boast, *I do my duty*, is the only one authorized to confidently say, *I demand*. When that day arrives we will know without reservation or disdain that government workers are not our bosses but our servants.

Here is the crux of the matter: Puerto Rico's most pressing problem is not one of education or of instruction, but of the people. We have a chessboard full of problems yet we concentrate on the large pieces: agriculture, health, commerce and political status, while the continental power of our opponent has us in a continuous state of checkmate. We have slowly but surely lost castles and bishops; we are confronted by a chessboard covered with pawns. When countries are accosted by political crises, economic ills or anything threatening their strength, those men and women who were raised stimulated by their culture are wont to fare far better than those whose spiritual mettle had not been forged in their formative years.

Our pawns with degrees, same as factory worker and field hand, don't have the skills to sort out situations for which their souls have never been prepared. The people expect everything from government and the government confides exclusively in its department of public education to shape minds. Yet, though it consumes close to half the budget, it is unable to assume responsibility for protecting music, letters, painting, popular art, public spaces, academies, museums, libraries, fairs, exhibitions and all those activities that fine-tune those senses that equip men's spirits with the resistance required to defend themselves in times of major collective crises.

Our school population numbers about 600,000 children. Forty percent of the island's budget dedicated to public education allows for the admittance of 115,000 children in urban schools and 125,000 in rural schools. Three hundred and sixty thousand children remain abandoned! One hundred thousand of those matriculated rural students attend class half a day for lack of teachers, space and equipment, proof that our financial powerlessness is casting a large incapacitated population adrift. Yet from here we will send out into the world the "self-made" men so badly formed from the very start.

The education department cannot do it all. It also cannot count on the many teachers betraying their vocations who, instead of honing characters, have made teaching a modus vivendi. No one is able to give what they do not have. Whosoever lacks the devotion to fulfill his mission after office hours, whosoever does not know how to master facts and figures and authoritatively rise above the dry subject he teaches, whosoever does not have the capacity to penetrate the virgin territories of a mind with a guiding light to free and channel latent potentials should, finally, resign their post. Teaching is something more than a mere profession; it is a difficult mission which cannot be fulfilled devotedly by someone who is only concerned with making a living.

With what authority can a teacher request his disciples to read something when he himself reads nothing? The scanty reading assignments given by so many teachers dash my hopes. From a book's perspective, some dwellings are splendid extensions of the desert. Their residents are on bad terms with meditation; it's why they find themselves with few means and poor resources. Slaves to their texts and course of study, they are neither able to hear the buzz of life outside the classroom nor hear the beating hearts that will soon be facing the future. No one can feel goodwill toward these inadequate teachers who are only interested in shaping pinheads. To make a living from children, to use them for profit is more than villainy. It deprives society of its best hopes.

The teaching profession in Puerto Rico, in terms of degrees, techniques and number, has advanced startlingly. Yet the impositions teachers suffer, with activities and tasks, are truly draining and are not compensated commensurately. Nevertheless their chief preoccupation is not the child per se, but their superiors; not the conscientious performance of duty to the changeable human demands of the group he or she directs, but the uniform requirements of principals and superintendents. The former is wanting in selective conditioning—sift and purge work—tending to the Socratic faculties of individual teachers. For the latter a teacher's certificate suffices and a bit of intellectual ability to comply with all the reasonable demands of the system. Instruction needs *teachers*, but teaching requires *educators*.

Another dismaying but unexplored subject among us is the dangerous monopoly women have over teaching jobs. According to the last census the male population in Puerto Rico is almost the same as the female. The total number of occupations is divided as follows: three quarters for men, one quarter for women. When it comes to schools the numbers are transposed. Men have been leaving this poorly compensated field and women scholars have been replacing them. Of the 4,639 teachers that served on the lines of public education this year (1932–33), 3,420 are women, that is to say, more than 73 percent.

The proportions seem staggering if one bears in mind the strategy, the protective armor and the aggressiveness that contemporary life demands of us. Women, by temperament, are gentler and less aggressive than men and have not been emancipated from superficial concerns yet. They have lived with fear and experienced the importance of appearances and, in general, are content to scratch things on the surface, not going deeper to the substance. Women pray for peace, not war; their element is lyric, not epic. Life seems more beautiful when they observe its pace at the bottom of a mirror. They are moved by the littlest things and their nervous systems are easily triggered.

I do not believe the braggart's silly propaganda about the inferiority of women. Neither do I believe in the traditional privileges of men that originate from social injustice and are soon to be completely revoked. All the same, I do believe in differing formative influences. There is a well of domesticity in women, instinctively maternal and emotional, that warrants their partial monopoly of positions in grammar schools. Men have a particular way of facing life, of colliding with it, of situating themselves in front of it that will build a student's character differently. This masculine approach should be considered without chauvinism or ineffectual substitutes in intermediate school and, most especially, in high school. Lest we forget, however, there are also useless men. These posts must be retained for forceful males only.

We are forced to direct attention, without hyperbole and in good faith, toward the courage and energy needed by the school's members, not only to form principals, but to recondition a body of persons that can form the basis for a new public ethic. For the great majority of women there are many areas of contemporary life that are still hermetically sealed off. Also if we add to this almost irremediable situation the mind-boggling problems of sex and the prickly reactions of feminine psychology, including touchiness, tears and a penchant for gossip, we judiciously point out an educational problem worthy of serious consideration.

Besides what women offer in the classroom, we must expect a more meaningful and serious collaboration from women than what they now contribute to the country. With the system of government currently in power she has walked away from her mindless work and isolation and ceased to be a decorative figure in the home. A few short years ago she obtained the right to vote from our legislature, and numerous prerogatives heretofore unknown to her are within her grasp today. It is no surprise that her interests now transcend fashion, possessions or the vote.

The extent of a woman's influence must include the home, which is the center of her universe. The demands of public life must not thwart the housewife or relegate the well-deserved attention home economics deserves to second place. Helping to shape the perfect mistress of the house, so responsible for native industry, agriculture and commerce, is a political—and very patriotic—mission we all share. Our tables, poor and exotic, are inclined to be abundant but not nutritious. They satiate but generally do not nourish. We import what the country can produce and therefore do not cooperate with our national economy. In order for the merchant's clarion call, "to consume what the land produces," to be successful, women ought to preoccupy themselves with raising genuine mistresses of the home. Women's organizations should be working from the inside out.

These days it is not such a strange thing to see women's groups come to life once every four years. When adding up what women have achieved by organizing, a few leap year groups with electioneering names come immediately to mind: Women Suffragists, Non-Partisan Women, Women Voters, Vanguard of Republican Women, and Women Liberals. It appears as though our women cannot unite outside a feverishly charged committee atmosphere.

Even during elections these same committees, as fond as any male group of speeches and budgets, destroy themselves with worse or identical pet peeves than men. After elections are over only the memory of political disagreements that gave them life remains, along with a few pictures in newspapers and magazines.

After an election look for what remains of the few seemingly effective women's groups. You will find a desolate vacuum. Our women leaders are content to speak at meetings and attain some positions for female members. A few flirt with cultural activities but on the whole are fonder of bridge parties, and also live for any news about the social set. They groom small ideas and squirrel away a few tried-and-true issues in their dressing tables. Every once in a while they agree upon a charitable event and that is all we have to be grateful for.

I do not refer to the homemaker, anchored in her house with the weight of maternal obligations, or to the furrowed laborer, in a permanent state of siege from hunger and her own limitations. Nor do I refer to the little miss of the house whose main preoccupations are the *thé dansant*, the car and a few words in English. I am referring to women intellectuals, influential organizers who gain public attention and are in a position to render better services to the culture. If these women cannot succeed in entering the deepest recesses of the people and the heart of our island, they should not regard my criticisms as cavalier. I beg the reader to keep in mind that I am not writing a madrigal.

What we need on the chess table of our problems is a bit of expertise and human sensibility to move the pieces. Come down out of the trees and get a feel for the realities of our diabetic island. "If we were as good at practicable activity as we are skilled and ingenious at conceptualization," noted Dr. José Padin, "this would be a paradise of prosperity like Jauja in Perú. At times I think we should declare a moratorium on ideas," Dr. Padin continues, "and dedicate ourselves for a time to putting into action a few of those brilliant concepts floating around intellectual circles."

We speak in terms of our country, yet we have sold her. We call ourselves Rico, that is to say rich, but we are poor. Sugar cane consumes us and is life giving. Coffee continues to be threatened by storms while tobacco is threatened by buyers. We can produce everything yet we even import meat and tomatoes. Corporations exploit us while they give food to the worker. Absentee ownership takes our riches and the country has no capital to replace them. Two languages are at odds though we cannot dispense with either. Every legislative session passes new laws and the municipal authorities are never placated. There are several things our farmers can depend on: miserable food credits, deprivation, tuberculosis, nepotism, high taxes, greatly diminished borrowing power, political dependence, party warfare, rising population, unskilled labor, large estate hold-ers, cronyism, storms, hurricanes, crises.

Yet in the presence of such chaos, which requires a practical spirit and much work, we are prepared to sit and wait for solutions from the outside. We allow others to do what falls upon us to do. This is why I believe our most serious problem is that of the people themselves, our most serious need the formation of a new Puerto Rican who knows how to frame and gauge our reality with fresh determination, without sugarcoating or confusion, but with a fit-ting, high-minded vision.

Let us save ourselves from falling upon that pointed verse from *Poema del Cid* with which Pedro Bermúdez challenges one of the Carrión infantes: "Tongue without hands, how dare you speak?"

Treading on these heels, I leave you with the warning given by the educator Tirso de Molina: "Vizcaíno is the iron I entrust to you/ poor in words, but rich in works."

Our Rhetoricalness

Rhetoricalness is not a characteristic unique to Puerto Rico. On many occasions Eugenio María de Hostos, among many others, has pointed it out as peculiar to Latin Americans. In assessing their feelings toward this double talk, Maríano Picón Salas has said, "rhetoric...is one of our continental vices, and such a dangerous vice that it colors all others, adorning them with tinsel... Tropicalism is an inability to call things by their proper names; a verbal delirium, a distortion of facts and ideas."

We, who have always lived immersed in grammar, have never been able to call things by their proper names. The Creole had no choice but resort to verbal as well as commercial contraband. Invasive inspections caused the people to develop skills in shrewdness and *jaibería*, the native symptomatic term meaning "intended malice," and our *jíbaro*, who exhibits these traits marvelously, had to look for the paths of least resistance in commerce and expression to mislead a Government whose distrustful vigilance zealously obstructed the few routes open to us. Our noun for shortcut, *atrecho*, and our verb for taking it, *atrechar*, are words born of Puerto Rican necessity, and still are not sanctioned by the Academy.* Their origins were secured by the first 300 years of Spanish education, during which time all we knew were *grammar teachers*, according

* Sanctioned by the Real Academia Española in 2001.

to sixteenth-century reports signed by the canon Torres Vargas in 1647 and authorized by Alejandro O'Reilly in 1765. Here lay the educational roots of our rhetoricalness.

Yet we need not go so far. I have not forgotten the noble efforts my teachers in North American public school made, not so long ago, to speak correctly, choosing as models the most difficult passages from *Don Quixote*. I remember as if it were yesterday the excessive praises sung at the burlesque and bombastic description of the first outing the nobleman of La Mancha pictured in his mind: "...apenas había el rubicundo Apolo tendido por la faz de la ancha y espaciosa tierra las doradas hebras de sus hermosos cabellos, y apenas los pequeños y pintados pajarillos, con sus arpadas lenguas..." (...hardly had the rubicund Apollo hung the golden tresses of his gorgeous hair on the wide, spacious earth and hardly had the tiny, speckled birdies with their harplike tongues...). And with this paragraph, inflated with such bad taste and classic Cervantes satire, they trained us in proper Spanish usage. God forgive them! Later I met with Cervantes in high school, through Hernandez's *Gramática*; the Puerto Rican author offered the paragraph as an exercise in the last chapter of his book. As an adult I came to realize the great error of all when I sat down to read *Don Quixote* thoughtfully for the first time. The least Cervantes-type paragraph was becoming, by art and grace of injected rhetoricalness, an exemplary model, a thing of beauty!

If we leap over the school fence into history and life, we will find an explanation for this verbose style, the political situation that more so than now kept our spirit imprisoned at the time. In the face of threatened confinement or banishment we repressed our intentions in a palpable concoction of speech consisting of vagueness, metaphor and circumlocution. Unfortunately, clarity and accuracy—those free routes—were hazardous to the genuine feelings that stirred within us. Seeking release they found shelter in the adjective and periphrasis, inevitably falling into a rhetoricalness that found its beginnings in the archaic education we received.

Colonial problems have weighed heavily upon the country and have driven the Creole to the sanctum of verbal hypocrisy, foraging for words to eloquently conceal opinions he could not fully express, worried about offending the oh-so-delicate sensibilities of the rulers. Excessive surveillance converted us into smugglers of contraband insular ideas. In this way we tackled problems with defensive tactics, walking through dangerous *atrechos*, stifling the soundless screams of our rebellious acts with agreeable words. With great care we went about hiding the sum of our meager intentions in the embellishment of paragraphs, in protective, superfluous verbosity, in formless clouds of words. In this shady manner we released, by stealth, our civic restlessness, but we also began to simultaneously develop a mind-set that has served to support the verbosity of the present day. This miserable prestidigitation in eloquence is a hundred years old and should always be seen for its protective function.

Around 1816 Juan Rodríguez Calderón wrote the first secular poem of known authorship, giving it the "short" and prophetic title "A la Hermosa y Feliz Isla de San Juan de Puerto Rico" (To the Beautiful and Happy Isle of San Juan de Puerto Rico). Many years later, José Gautier Benítez proclaimed, "bello jardín de América el ornato, siendo el jardín América del mundo." (America is the world's garden, while you are the choicest flower in the garden of America the beautiful). We are in the middle of poetic rubbish and the examples are hundredfold. The quotation is indicative of these plainly understood flattering portraits. Then the ungrateful foreigner, the poet Manuel del Palacio, wrote the uncomplimentary sonnet about us which begins: "This place that centuries ago was a Rich Port/Today should be called Poor Port/Since whosoever searches for gold there or silver or copper/Is the sure owner of old sovereigns equal one pound sterling." It goes on to mention the realities of our inertia, heat, illegitimate children, blacks and the stew we eat called *mofongo*. But José Gualberto Padilla, (a.k.a. El Caribe), answered Del Palacio with a paraphrased sonnet and a long, popular composition that fills fourteen pages. No less of a response was warranted. The incident occurred in 1873 but the inverse happened about 1912 when the poet Santos Chocano arrived in Puerto Rico and dedicated his very celebrated poem "La ciudad encantada" (The Enchanted City) to San Juan. The poem also began his book, *Puerto Rico Lírico* (Lyric Puerto Rico). The entire country knew how to repay the Poet of America's gallant, rhetorical outpour with their money and their gratitude. Previously we had done the same with Salvador Rueda, and later with Francisco Vallaespesa.

For forty years we have passionately discussed in the press, books and the theater the unequivocal location of where Columbus landed as if this heated and long debate was enormously important to the spiritual life of the people. Even I could not help adding my two cents in *Aristas,* my book of essays, where I also voiced my rhetorical support to another overworked controversy regarding whether or not we should say *portorriqueño* or *puertorriqueño*. There is no lack of fireworks at our festivities.

We debate with ceremonial grimness, hopelessly and histori- cally addicted to discursiveness. We have adjusted the course of life to the pace of our militant imagination and we pronounce our civic aspirations in a Castelarian tone. We cannot disavow Castelar, our great lyric uncle. Moreover, a voluminous work of our political his- tory can be written from conversations at banquers alone and referenced with thousands of like-minded telegrams. The dining room and the telegraph have played reprehensible roles in the for- mation of the verbal homeland, airways always open to relieve the congestion of our endemic rhetorical dropsy. Instead of setting his- tory on fire, we set the words that can topple empires on fire. Out of a country of 1.5 million, only two dozen names constitute what the press calls the "Voice of the Nation." The rest of us have no voice...or vote. The voice of public opinion falls to a few. How many programs and resolutions haven't come out of those dens of rhetoricalness where barbers and pill dispensers preside! The bar- bershop and drugstore contain the perfect conditions for caucus- ing. In every town both join to form a type of Associated Press through which all municipal and insular life circulate to the point of insinuation. The sounds of cutting shears and pill pushing underscore agreements and resolutions, conceived a little at a time in backbiting contention. These resolutions attempt to ward off, by work and grace of the divine verb, the national crisis with an oral thrashing. For the most part, our political *caciques* are men skilled with shaving cream or poultices.

The razor blade and spatula proffer their stupendous collaboration to insular policy. The barbershop and pharmacy are close to harboring political orators and committees. They take to heart excessive liberties with their "sacred love of the Puerto Rican homeland." I am avoiding, for the moment, other social problems whose origins and development are found in both places, and I will substantiate my best of intentions when I refer to them later in this essay.

After all is said and done, what will our *prohombres* do in those gloomy towns deep in the interior, closed to all nonpartisan stimulation and benumbed by the ritornello of endless commissions traveling to Washington, D.C.? What else can they do but extemporize, if for a moment, over our fate? What, if not to creatively sustain their big city dreams of good citizenship? Similarly that program proclaiming "the best men for the best jobs," which in reality loses all discriminating sense plus the desperate exaltation: "Give me independence, even if we die of hunger," reflect the recurrent notions of an internal government overextended with far-reaching fantasies of change. Tomás Carrión Maduro asserts that "islanders have invested the most precious part of their lives into a rhetorical army." From this lighthouse we mount a praetorian guard equipped with stores of imagination and sophistry.

When the historic Union Party of Puerto Rico was founded at the beginning of the twentieth century, someone pejoratively called it "a party of hot air," to which someone else answered, "Right, the hot air that will steam power and start up our great family's boat." From the socialist fuse, the beak of the republican eagle and the trunk of the coalitionist elephant the road to hell was easily paved with the deluge of dense phrases that fell like stones over the people. In the middle of the Chamber of Representatives our recently handicapped distinguished writer and poet José De Diego— who became lame toward the end of his life—proposed the lame-brained idea that the island of Puerto Rico had to be divided into seven districts "because there were seven colors in the rainbow, seven wonders of the world, seven capital sins, seven days in a week," etc. The humorist Canales answered De Diego by asserting there had to be four districts because there were four cardinal points, four legs on a horse, four corners in a table.

This special mode of behavior does not begin with our honorable "Captain General Excellencies," nor with the "very loyal and very noble city of San Juan Bautista de Puerto Rico." It is part of our racial inheritance, passed on to us with the pompous name of the island, born in a momentary explosion of joy, in a period when the power of sixteenth-century sophisms predominated. With the same haste with which we now seek to resolve our serious problems with trite phrases, we were unsuitably christened and we have carried the name like a golden cross upon the weak shoulder of our misfortune. Our first lesson in rhetoric was taught by the edge of a baptismal font when we were christened *Puerto Rico* (Rich Port).

Our sparse mines were stripped completely in the first few years of the conquest. We have been reduced since then to our current state of poverty, and it has increased with each successive period by a series of, at times, variable yet permanent circumstances. Our poor physical constitution, vacillating industry and anemic lives have not been seen by a world distracted by the lyric pomp of our name. The panorama of *Boriquen's* misery has a centennial perspective. As far back as one can remember our *jíbaro*, our laborer, eats poorly, lives poorly, works hard and makes very little money. Hurricanes, earthquakes and epidemics aggravate, time and again, our permanent economic instability, and beneath the rhetorical exuberance of an adjective, we trudge along with our bitter existence despite our vegetative weariness. As if this were not enough, the tourist—globetrotter without a conscience or eyes to see—helps to conceal our misery by flatteringly referring to us as the Enchanted Island, the Pearl of the Antilles, the American Switzerland.

On the other hand, Puerto Rico's surrounding islands, small and barren, do not partake of this metaphoric optimism. The geographic nomenclature ascribed to them honestly expresses our reality: *Caja de Muerto* (Coffin Island), *Desecho* (Scrap Island), *Mona* (Monkey Island), *Monito* (Little Monkey Island), *Pata de Cabra*

(Goat's Foot), *Culebra* (Snake Island). Eduardo Zamacois, during a trip to Puerto Rico, visited the little island, *Pata de Cabra*, which lies in the mouth of El Morro. Its welcoming leper colony offered a macabre salutation to visitors, and Zamacois' book, *La Alegria del Andar* (The Joy of Sailing), devoted a chapter to it, justifiably called *"La Isla del Espanto"* (Fright Island).

Our prolific capacity for embellishment has centripetal force. It excludes the surrounding sea, but manifests itself strongly within our shores beginning with the unfulfilled aspirations of our humble towns huddled beneath the flattering shade of bombastic tropes with names such as: *La Ciudad Encantada* (The Enchanted City), *Perla del Sur* (Pearl of the South), *Sultana del Oeste* (Sultan of the West), *Ciudad del Turabo* (Turabo City, exotic name of an indigenous village), *del Plata* (Silver City), *del Guamani* (Guamani City, another indigenous toponym), *de las Lomas* (City of Small Hills).

Barros changed its name to Orocovis and I have seen proposals in the press to change the name of the island to Luis Muñoz Rivera and to change Mayagüez to Hostos. Rhetoric and poetry! Everything here tends to solve itself to the rhythm of the American National Anthem or our own "La Borinqueña."

Our people harbor an atavistic enthusiasm for sophistry. Rather than love the efficiency of the well-timed word, they are enraptured by words in symphonic droves. I have mentioned previously that circumlocution for us is something of a strategy worked out in the trenches where we have had to defend our positions for hundreds of years. A people who have found themselves in an interminable trial by jury have to pace themselves to the rhythms of juridical argument.

The law is a contagious periphrastic profession that strongly attracts the interest of Puerto Rican youth. No other profession functions better on the basis of technicalities. A comma, word or phrase can completely change the spirit of the law and can become the grounds for arguments often favoring a guilty party or endangering an innocent one. The technicality is in its environment in so-called parliamentary laws. Points of order, prior matters and personal privilege are the most ferocious adversaries of men of good-will. I have never seen greater disorders than those caused by a point of order. We speechify amongst ourselves and have reduced an excellent activity into a tasteless display because some go to meetings not to discuss, or reason discreetly and selflessly, but to win the applause of dolts or, what's worse, to hear themselves speak.

We are a country of know-it-alls. Tempests and earthquakes have not caused as much damage to our character as that avalanche of sudden experts who infallibly explain their causes and effects in the press. Without the least hesitation, we invent atmospheric and geological theories. Improvisation is our forte. The assertion "I'm not prepared" by a speaker is, in the end, a two-hour discourse. These lay pronouncements tend to consolidate public opinion into a *Boricua* we know today as the "statement." The statement is a turn to defend yourself and serves to incite all the social gatherings in the country. The statement can turn into a dialogue and become synthesized in a publication such as *Interview*; other times it acquires significance and becomes part of *Manifiesto*. When sprinkled with indulgent frivolity the statement is reduced to the vilest plebeian category and printed in *Crónica Social*.

Crónica Social seems to have been invented just for us; it is the sewer for our rhetoricalness, our words laid waste under the weight of its foolishness. Who isn't familiar with the impotent, affected vocabulary of our social pages? Who hasn't felt spiritually nauseated when reading so much garbage of interest only to those mentioned in the column? These pages suffer from the same thing the renowned name of Puerto Rico suffers from. They are false gems, illusions, deliberate misrepresentations, prestidigitations that artfully conceal our etiology.

We have learned how to sugarcoat a pill perfectly. Laziness masquerades as indolence or unemployment, crime as homicide. Words like "cheat" and "thief" gradually fall out of usage; when discussing someone who uses money not their own, terms like "irregularities," and "misapplication" or "diversion of funds" are used. "What a fall from grace!" we all declare sympathetically. We call the professional drunkard "someone who can complete a party of guests," and we qualify the woman who smokes, drinks and is

always on the go as "modern." We whitewash the scoundrel or malefactress because what matters is concealing shape and form. Just as we sugarcoat the pill, we sugarcoat our lives.

Living for the sake of appearance is another graphic form of this habit, which however universal it may be, is pitiable in us. A French scientist, Pierre Ledru, visited the island at the end of the eighteenth century and effortlessly caught us in the spectacle of being ourselves. In his *Journey to the Island of Puerto Rico*, published in 1797, the explorer says: "Many colonists, hardly blessed with good fortune, still deprive themselves from ordinary pleasures for as long as six months, so they may distinguish themselves during the first races through their elegant dress and beautiful horse harnesses." This observation is still valid today and the habit is aggravated by the greater extension of credit. We dress and live by the installment plan, veneering our lives with each installment, sliding down the income tightrope in a continuous and dangerous balancing act lest we fall. The same phenomenon occurs in our Treasury Department, burdened by government loans, taxes and in a permanent state of crisis. Our monocultivated country forces a large population into a brutal human competition; labor is cheapened and unemployment inevitable. The power of acquisition will keep up with the need of distribution. Since having possessions and paying debts are not easily juggled and we want, even need, to sustain our social prestige by seeming to live comfortably, we lower the curtain of credit on our private scene—rice and two-wheeled carriages—until having come to ruin, bankruptcy or the "accidental" fire destroys the fake decor. An excursion through the records of insurance companies and registry of deeds may well hurl a huge dose of acid over the plated veneer of our social positions. Our fourteen-karat rhetoricalness vanishes with the gentlest rub of a legal investigation.

In this manner we go about our lives. Our rhetoricalness has already clamored on for forty years. This venal bravado that toys with the true misery of our surrounding reality is extremely dangerous and sad despite its happy façade.

Patriotism as "sport" must be eliminated, at least the vulgar, bombastic notion that here is called patriotism. We have lived with palms turned upward asking for what is already ours, allowing others to read our fortune and predict a shining future. The time has come to live with fists prepared to confront all those who cheapen patriotic sentiment with hollow words. A well-aimed, collective blow to the mouth will remove the homeland from our lips so that we, then, might be able to give it asylum in our hearts.

The Dutchman Will Catch Us

an almost uniform parallelogram surrounded by a ripped necklace of tiny islets, Puerto Rico lies between the Caribbean Sea and the Atlantic Ocean, an inhospitable place for soirées, to be sure. It is the smallest of the Greater Antilles, and continuing guardianships and executors have maintained it in an inviolable state of adolescence for centuries. This extended childhood prolonged to the present day, and overseen by mandatory governesses has forced us to obey rules that restrict our friendships with the other Antilles, and consequently from confraternity with Latin America and the rest of the globe. We have not yet come of age and this separates us from the world.

Our marvelous geographical position, much touted today as an aerial traffic hub between North America and South America and a possible bridge between two new-world cultures, has never received from the Spanish government the favor conferred at other times upon Cuba and the Dominican Republic. These sister Antilles were more accessible and important to colonial development. We remained at the margins of European routes, embedded in a centuries-old isolation that always frustrated our yearning to be a part of Indo-America. Imprecise and mistaken maps such as

Mercator's Map of 1625, Samson's Map of 1657 and 1697, and Juillet's Map of 1703 aided and abetted our inevitable banishment. Around 1791 a new, plausible map that corrected the principal faults and errors was published in Madrid by Tómas López. Despite its defects this was the best map published prior to the nineteenth century. At times we have not even been recorded on maps and have existed at the mercy of careless cartographers—consequences of our negligible size. Do I make my case?

In the October 1930 issue of *Present Day American Literature*, dedicated to Puerto Rico, Harriet Wagner is absolutely correct in stating, "They [the schoolchildren] have an unusual interest in faraway places and enjoy going to the map." Besides the natural interest unknown lands awaken in children, this childlike attitude holds all the melancholy of unceasing isolation that soothes itself through an unusual interest in geography classes. The map we admire and study affectionately is a secret escape valve through which our unconscious migratory pressure is released.

During the initial thirty years of colonization the first drastic laws were passed to prohibit anyone from leaving the island. México and Perú, with their extraordinary riches, incited old settlers on the island to liberating emigrations they were unable to complete. According to historian Salvador Brau, "To Governor Obando [these laws] were necessary to prevent the island from becoming uninhabited. Whosoever attempted to take their leave would be threatened with hanging. Even so, some secretly escaped to the isle of Mona. The hardy governor was forced to pursue them, flogging some and opening gashes on the bottom of others' feet in an attempt to contain them."

Restrained to the rock by the memories of these wounds, we remained paralyzed and feeble within our own island frontiers until the nineteenth century when a truly historical event took place. Several young Puerto Rican men, with the help of Father Rufo, left Puerto Rico, later to return from Spain with degrees, teaching in our country's schools until the governor unconscionably divested them of their professorships arbitrarily. Even today the story told by the Puerto Rican, Alonso Ramirez, of how he broke the Confinement Laws and victoriously sailed around the world in the seventeenth century is astounding.

The conquests of México and Perú were magnets for colonial traffic while Puerto Rico lagged behind in terms of maritime movement. Weak foreign commerce was limited to ports in Cádiz, Seville and San Juan, and communication was so infrequent that the presence of ships at port were a reason for the city's jubilation. On May 20, 1662 military camp commander Juan Pérez de Guzmán affirmed that no merchant ship from Spain had stopped in Puerto Rico in eleven years. In *Puerto Rican Miscellany* by Pedro de Angelis we stumble upon this heart-sickening statement: "The arrival of a small ship loaded with merchandise from St.Thomas was such a novelty! What commotion and liveliness...! Any time a ship approached, the city would come back to life as if a genuine party or plenary indulgence had been proclaimed by the pope. At the time St.Thomas was our Paris or Liverpool in these matters." Such an occurrence, clamorously announced for all to hear as people gathered at the bay shouting enthusiastically, "Ships! Ships!" provided a lively interval during the impenetrable isolation in which the colony lived.

Other coastal towns, cut off by governmental decree, could not share this happy sight in the capital city. By the time other parts began to open with official sanction it was too late. Our needs forced us to clandestinely penetrate all coasts without the Government's knowledge.

We lived in isolation. "It was not uncommon," according to José G. del Valle, "for the most important town events to be known in San Juan one month after having occurred, and the arrival of mail from Spain, or a foreign ship with correspondence constituted an extraordinary event and was the talk of the people for days."

Lack of good roads connecting to San Juan, the ease with which goods could be exchanged at unwatched coasts, and preferences for foreign merchandise since they were superior to and cheaper than Spanish products drove our hedged-in colony to contraband activity. It served to cheer our dismal state for many years. Mocking tariffs through illegal commerce gave us a great big window on the world's progress. Its enormous usefulness was discreetly recorded in the renowned *Reports of Alejandro O'Reilly,* when he wrote in 1765: "During the day they [Puerto Ricans] pay in advance for some other little thing that stimulates the sale of fruits by foreigners and the rivalry with which the foreigners placed them along with plaids, Brittany cloth, handkerchiefs, hemp and flax fabrics, hats and all sorts of goods they introduce, so that this illegal trade, which in most of the Americas is so detrimental to the king's interest and Spain's commerce, has been useful here." Seclusion compelled us to initiate contraband relationships, unknown to San Juan authorities, the only official port open to the world's friendship.

Through this one sanctioned, narrow opening passed the only cultural forces of the last century, as well as thousands of immigrants that significantly increased our population. We took in both at this opportune time, but despite their valuable contributions neither mitigated the general reticence of our day. I remember as a youth living in a town in the interior of the island, when a trip to San Juan was considered a genuine event. During his many visits to the countryside in 1927, philologist Tomás Navarro Tomás met many souls who had never stepped outside the rural confines of their homes. On the other hand it can doubtless be said that the majority of Puerto Ricans do not have even a middling knowledge of Puerto Rico. This observation, which would make sense in larger countries, has unique implications within our small geographic area, today covered by such fine roads. It is also true that with modern commuting conveniences our apathy toward travelling to the interior has diminished a bit, but not enough to assert that we know ourselves fully. With regard to foreign countries it can still be said that with the exception of travel northward, we ignore international routes, recoiling our soles from the smarting memory of bloodletting provoked by our first migratory attempts. When analyzed from a cultural point of view this attitude's full problematic dimension speaks for itself.

Just yesterday we were discussing the problem of Spanish

schools; today we talk of North American schools. We have adopted a compliant attitude. Puerto Rican schools have remained a pending subject on our list of priorities despite their inability to imbue the atmosphere with what it should to buoy up the soul of a people. If the soul is a product of the schools and the schools are a product of the soul, neither has been able to come together and grow within the necessary conditions of full sovereignty whose only allegiance is to the will of the people. Underage, isolated and obedient to continental orders that superseded our own wishes, this remote island has never been able to answer cultural invitations the world has addressed to us. Obligated to turn a deaf ear to these calls, we remain in this Caribbean municipality, holding on to dreams of progress and international exchange so as to fulfill the historical mission we ourselves are capable of accomplishing without a foreign power determining it for us.

There are various theories regarding the special mission of islands. Ripped from the heart of continents, stormy seas indefinitely prolonged their separation. Optimistic dogma attributes glorious deeds far greater than what islands historically have performed. They were geographically destined to be anchored environments used for various political and economic strategies. From Plato's resonating Atlantis to the latest contemporary treatises, island literature has glossed over the tragic anguish in which island life unfolds with panegyric and solemn pomposity.

That important thinker from Granada, Ángel Ganivet, noting the European influence on the territorial spirit, cuts a suit far too large to fit us. Surely he must have been thinking of England when he wrote the following in his book *Idearium*: "In comparing the specific dispositions of diverse social groups, we find them assuming the inherent qualities of their territories; resistance is characteristic of continental peoples while aggression is characteristic of islanders...The islander understands that isolation solidifies his defense; he would accept foreign domination only if he lacks the power to maintain his independence, but is in fact dependent, and knows moreover that the distinctiveness of his island's soil is so compelling that foreign components introduced to it will soon feel the pull of self-determination."

Ever since we appeared before the discovering eyes of the naval admiral, our island has been a politically juridical extension of the continent. When through time the continental transplantation acquired its own distinguishing marks and the assimilation of different cultures and races, a native feature rooted in the subsoil of this isle was created. The newly formed *Boricua* did not show signs of displacement and aggression as specific traits, but rather recalcitrance and inflexibility as defense mechanisms. Since we never participated directly in establishing international relations, through which commerce and culture would have expanded our mental outlook, we have remained hemmed in at the center, unable to stretch our limbs and breathe the air of other countries. Well into the nineteenth century our solitariness was harrowing.

In 1831 Pedro Tomás de Córdoba states, in his superb *Memoirs*, "The multitude of pirates that infested these waters totally ruined the mercantile industry and we had hardly progressed agriculturally. Business was stagnant and a paralysis of the body politic made the running of government difficult, producing the rapid deterioration the island fell into until 1824." Stagnation, paralysis, difficulties, deterioration—here are the consequences of our tragic isolation. Puerto Rico's "...virtual lack of communication with other Spanish colonies," says Marcelino Menéndez y Pelayo, "suffices to explain the absence of literary traditions for three centuries."

Our strongest defense was not to be found in seclusion, as Ganivet believes. Open on all four sides to adventurous avarice and conquest, the island was easy pickings for pirates and international expeditions, and because Spain's naval power did not dominate these waters we had to defend ourselves by moving inland. Later we ended up an insignificant possession compared to the very rich Aztec and Incan empires. Though the island was propitious for invasion, it was never fit to be invaded. Isolation and territorial size have condemned us to live in continuous submission, using as our defense not aggression, but a patience that characterizes our many civil protestations.

Isolation blocks all discourse, cuts us off from the body of intellectual fellowship and distances us from new trends and ideas that are stirring the conscience of the world today. Our solitude still constitutes one of the most repressive vestiges of our culture and an explanatory factor for our fossilized personality. Officially, we live within a perpetual trust, living and breathing according to laws and statutes. We are born into, and grow up within, a colony. We think and act as a colony, expecting a homeland by prescription. Our vital statistics fluctuate between two extraterritorial points: Madrid and Washington. Our pulse has been taken from such distances with doctor's orders arriving from both places. Our national temperature has been conditioned by historical, not tropical, climates. Waiting for word from these capitals we ignore the rest of the world. Royal decrees and congressional laws have been the magnetic focus of our attention. All else seems superfluous to us.

Puerto Rico has lived a fictitious historical life, foreign to its ethnic nature, forced to react reflexively to events and stimuli borne outside our collective conscience. Vigilant foreign legislation imposes an unnatural order upon Puerto Rico's civic behavior, and in the face of these limiting boundaries she has had to orient her nature to styles alien to her: the Court at Cádiz for one and the European War for another. Constant disciplinary guardianships have reconditioned our differentiating characteristics (on one occasion a governor forbade mustaches) and we have had to internalize our focus, concentrating on our own person, abandoning completely the contemplation of countries surrounding us. Puerto Rico's history has had to develop defensively, falling back on herself, keeping to herself to avoid strategic mistakes. To defend ourselves against pirates we walled in the capital city, and though the walls were torn down in 1897 to facilitate urban sprawl we have nevertheless been unable to destroy the psychological walls standing in the way of cultural growth. In 1644 the bishop of Puerto Rico, Damián López de Haro, wrote: "We are so besieged by enemies here that Puerto Ricans dare not step into a boat to fish, for fear the

Dutch will catch them straightaway." This statement still holds true. The pirates who kept us hemmed in—it must be said once and for all—were not always Dutch. What is true is that we have not spoken our piece for fear that the "Dutchman" will still catch us.

More and more the arms of the sea that created us and oppress us prevent us from seeing the pageantry of the world, narrowing our appreciative vision while proportionately widening our local vision. Drawn inward, crushed by a dense population of 485 inhabitants per square mile, we live impassively, united in our abulia, believing we are the center of the world, wedged in this corner of the Antilles, far from the rhythm of all Latin American life. Ruled by the recurrent compass of expectation, we remain in a permanent state of uncertainty, not finding the definitive course of action though which our dreams may be materialized. The latest trend, proclaiming our mission as one of interpreters for two new-world cultures due to our geographical position and Anglo-Hispanic splicing, sets us up as diplomatic arbitrators, amicus curiae, working mediators in the acrimonious intercontinental debate. The mission is altruistic as long as we do not risk becoming a bridge everyone can step on, yet we are telephone, experimental lab, Pan-American traffic police and passive link in a chain. We will have to accept all these unless we react, demanding in exchange respect for our own inclinations, so as not to thwart the free and natural emergence of *boricuísmo*, which in the long run will be an authentic contribution to the culture.

Standing by for official word has prevented us from listening to our own inner voice so we can discover and cultivate the way of life that suits our best interests. So it is for the young to elucidate our most important needs, to peel off layers of the basic, common ideas that keep us stuck within a collective barrier, to find in the inner recesses of our life those solid points on which our personality is strengthened and, disregarding the noisy growing pains that accompany peoples in gestation, to hurl and scatter the seeds of our productive essence over official walls. This move is the remedy that will shed light upon our destiny and reduce our reticence when facing the universal concerns so instrumental for cultural achievement.

Insular*ismo*

A capacity for open-mindedness, expansion, growth and mental cosmopolitanism will force us to abandon the crypt of our political and economic prostration. A little exercise—an apprenticeship outside these walls—will do away with our inflexibility. The duty of Puerto Rico's youth is to tear down the wall of this isolation and take a good look around.

In order for the world to know us and galvanize us we must cease to be Robinson Crusoe. Let us go out to fish, though the Dutchman may catch us. One day we may return with our nets full!

A Ray
of Hope

Puerto Rican Affirmation

osendo Matienzo Cintrón, one of the most methodical minds we have produced, wrote in 1903: "Today Puerto Rico is nothing more than a throng. But when this throng obtains its soul, then Puerto Rico will be a homeland." Thirty years have come and gone and the situation has not improved.

After completing depressing research regarding the uncertainty of these days, first-rate minds fire off pessimistic conclusions from present murky circumstances. Mariano Abril, official historian of Puerto Rico, agrees: "But...does a soul exist? A Puerto Rican one? A surgeon would not find it with a scalpel; a psychologist would have his doubts. The country has come unhinged...like *Knight, Death and the Devil,* painted by the great Dürer, who hid the mere skin and bones of a haggard man behind splendid armor." Nobody should expect a surgeon, regardless of his expertise, to be able to find the soul of a people upon an operating table. We honestly believe a Puerto Rican soul does exist, luminous but latent, divided and dispersed, fragmented like a frustrated puzzle that has never enjoyed the full sense of its wholeness. We began its creation during the last century of our history, but the twists and turns of our political fate prevent us, to this day, from continuing this course of action.

Three centuries of quiet, slow navigation were not sufficient to find the route to *El Dorado*. We did catch a glimpse through the foggy coast of our collective consciousness in the nineteenth century, but just as we prepared to shout joyously: "Homeland, ho!" a warring hand broke our hold of the helm and our ship was left to drift.

We should not believe we are already fully grown. Sufficient time has not passed to create our definitive personality. "In order to create a people like the French—to create that community of thoughts and feelings that make up their soul—more than ten centuries were needed," says Gustavo Le Bon. Can we pretend to create ours in only one century when the monumental disadvantage of not being the masters of our own fate prevails? The homeland and the soul, free of provisional encumbrances, lie ahead of us. Here is a goal for sound young men and women.

As we have already indicated, the first three centuries of our history constituted a suckling period. We saw the world for the first time while tied to the apron strings of the conquering nation. Later we began to crawl, stumbling and hurting ourselves. As the nineteenth century began we took our first steps in the field of culture with marked difficulty.

When the motherland lost her American children and observed the wayward character of our sister Cuba, we then became to the Spaniards in Europe the *enfant gaté*, the favored child of the already shrinking Hispanic family. To the recalcitrant and obstinate Spaniards living here, we were disobedient, ungrateful and disloyal because we were beginning to object to the unjust treatment we received from these unfit foster parents, the general governors and their henchmen. We owe our strongest manifestations of Puerto Rican nationalism mainly to their despotic attitudes. How do we effectuate the change?

Three historic events indirectly inspire us to tend to our budding expression in the nineteenth century: the French Revolution, the American Revolution and the South American wars for independence. But the triumph of liberalism in Spain had a direct bearing upon the island and started us on our way.

The face of Ramón Power must be added to the anonymous

masses already sparking protests for Latin American solidarity. In 1810 Antonio Ignacio Cortabarría arrived in Puerto Rico "possessing special powers to arrange the end of discord in Venezuela," according to Brau. This commissioned officer considered it prudent to direct the peacemaking operation from Puerto Rico and even considered a possible auxiliary force made up of the island militia, but he had to rectify this presumption upon finding a defiant proclamation on the door of his house, stating: "We, the people, docile enough to obey the local authorities, will never tolerate sending even one militiaman to fight against our brothers in Caracas." This is a significant event. In a struggle between Spaniards and Venezuelans, Puerto Ricans sided with the latter. Future history, full of revolutions and military uprisings, will prove that the country no longer considers itself a stagnant extension of Spain, as it had during the first three centuries, but rather a part of America. We begin to be something else.

A priest, a journalist and an educator awaken us from the doldrums of three centuries and resurrect our dissatisfaction when his remedial measures were denounced. Father José Antonio de Bonilla, an authority on canonical law and theology, watched over the values of the Puerto Rican family, courageously battling monetary payments made for matrimonial dispensations. "No sooner do I make my plans known in Mayagüez in 1814 *in favor of my countrymen,*" he says in his book, "when insults, dishonor, defamation and opprobrium were heaped upon me, these being the thanks... evangelical ministers opposing the torrent of corrupt practices contrary to the spirit of religious law received immediately..." For defending us he was incarcerated and deported to Barcelona. He returned in 1823, and upon publishing his *Apuntamientos críticos* (Critical Notes) over the same incident was again persecuted, and emigrated to the Dominican Republic where he died penniless, after having served the Church for more than seventy years.

In that period from 1822 to 1823 liberalism triumphed in Spain, and new newspapers began to appear that, notwithstanding their short lives, cautiously recorded the anguish of a people in formation. In a beautiful gesture of growing solidarity upon Father

Bonilla's return, an article welcoming him back appeared in *El Eco* (The Echo). "Indeed, all *Puerto Ricans worthy of the name* congratulate you, our most esteemed Bonilla and we wish you tranquility, peace and quiet in the bosom of your homeland, your family and all your compatriots. They cordially congratulate you for having triumphed over your assassins..." This taunt, though unfair, is symptomatic and acquires tragic significance sometime afterward.

El Diario Económico in 1814 and *El Diario Liberal y de Variedades de Puerto Rico* in 1822 harbored timid Puerto Rican protests within their pages, but as they became less interdicted the protestations slowly became more deliberate. In the April 28, 1822 edition of *El Diario Liberal* we find a letter signed with three initials beginning as follows: "Beloved Puerto Rican compatriots: I speak to you all since this question at least applies to all and touches us all. Are we or are we not Spaniards, equal in every way to those on the peninsula, beloved motherland to which we belong? Are we or are we not all governed under the same laws and constitutional system?" This polite and fainthearted way of indicating existing inequities did not last long.

At about this time the first Puerto Rican journalist, José Andino de Amézquita, addressed a "letter to the electorate" in which the schism between Spaniards in Europe and Spaniards here is formed. Andino recommended the electorate vote for candidates born in Puerto Rico. Lieutenant Colonel Pedro Vasallo protests because Andino "has offended persons worthy of respect and consideration...and has a tendency to set up dividing lines, not only between Puerto Rican Spaniards and other Spaniards in the empire, but also between different classes of Puerto Rican Spaniards."

A courageous rejoinder from Andino reaffirming his previous recommendation appears in the March 27, 1823 edition of Puerto Rico's daily newspaper, *El Eco*. Despite his seventy years of age he cast a number of vehement aspersions at the lieutenant colonel. José Andino de Amézquita jump-starts the nervous system of our journalism, a defender of our personality since its inception. Like Bonilla and Power, Andino discovers the Creole nature. Little by little the island laboriously begins to appear, endowing us with the oils that will one day serve to paint her portrait.

The struggle for our rights continues in this manner. Our first intermediate school, *Seminario Conciliar (Theological Seminary)*, opened its doors in 1832. It begins functioning under the rectorate of a Puerto Rican, Friar Ángel de la Concepción Vázquez. Besieged by mishaps, he makes a devastating statement a few years later in a letter to the reputable Father Rufo. "I can do no less than say what I have always felt, education for youngsters on this island is under some kind of curse that presents formidable obstacles to confound and destroy it on all fronts..." Our people waged an uphill battle against official indifference that appeared to intentionally neglect education. Within the six voluminous books that make up the *Geographical, Historical, Economic and Statistical Reports on the Island of Puerto Rico* (published 1831–33 by Pedro Tomás de Córdoba) there is no mention of public education. It would have been a miracle and a falsehood.

Yet the name of Rafael Cordero, a brilliant black man, is recorded in our history as one whose artisan's desk was surrounded by children of all social classes to receive free instruction. Finally, note the extent of our vicissitudes during the first fifty years of this century with regard to the luck of a project created by the patriotic Economic Society of Friends of the Country, an organization promoting grammar school and high school instruction. In 1844 the society started a fund to build and maintain the *Colegio Central* (Central Grammar School), and in less than a month "was able to secure contributions in the amount of $30,000." According to José Julián Acosta, "Puerto Rican patriotism allocated the funds directly toward the realization of such a meritorious project." The project was endorsed by the Count of Mirasol, governor and captain general of the island. What followed still happens to this day: a change in administration. His excellency, Juan de la Pezuela, who did not approve the project, ordered all contributions returned. There never was a Central Grammar School.

This failure, however, did reap some benefit. In order to fill teacher posts in the school, the unforgettable Father Rufo was able to get four young Puerto Ricans to be sent to Spain to complete their studies in core subjects. Two of these four, Román Baldorioty de Castro and José Julián Acosta, were generously aided by Father Rufo. The two graduates returned seven years later only to find no school or means to employ their talent and diligence. On the other hand they brought with them a new desire and purpose that in time would strengthen our position.

Friar Ángel was right when he wrote his assessment [regarding the cursed state of Puerto Rican education]. The teaching posts in agriculture, navigation and botany, created by the Board of Commerce and Development, were filled by Baldorioty and Acosta. Yet when a new governor, Laureano Sanz, arrived in Puerto Rico he created dossiers on both teachers and they were fired from their teaching posts, losing in addition their personal rights, acquired with such great difficulty. This is how Spaniards hoped to exterminate the reformist ideas of our young people.

The development of education in this century is vitiated by suspicion, a lack of confidence, political fanaticism and rampant favoritism that disregarded the law and impeded the measures agreed to. Upper echelons in Spanish government had approved measures to build primary and secondary schools, agricultural colleges, and teachers colleges, none of which were carried out. A lack of resources was professed over here, although a palace for the Jesuits worth 200,000 *pesos* was being erected at the time. In order to be admitted to the Mother of the Sacred Heart School, liberally subsidized by the government, students had to provide documents with the "seal of the Holy Crusade, have meats at their disposal, plus 200 *pesos* a year." Religious groups, with support from the government and staffed almost entirely by European Spaniards, were solely responsible for education as a whole.

In 1875 the Provincial Deputation, elected by popular vote, created the first Civilian Institute of Puerto Rico. Despite rigorous Spanish opposition, the majority of teaching posts went to the country's sons and daughters educated in Spain. However, when the reactionary General Sanz returned for a second time to Puerto Rico, he abolished the Deputation, duly elected by the people, and appointed another of his own choosing. He also abolished the Civilian Institute, arranging for students to be transferred to the Jesuit school to finish their studies. He dismissed Puerto Rican teachers of the Institute in order to fill their posts with Spaniards, and even prohibited private instruction without prior authorization to make sure the dismissed civil servants would starve to death.

The painful process of our development as a new people, with dignity, was misconstrued by the government as genuine anti-Spanish sentiment, the specter with which they defended and supported their excesses before the central government. Let us say, for the sake of accuracy, that hostile feelings toward Spain per se did not exist in Puerto Rico. However, hostility did exist toward her colonial policies. The contempt and injustice with which Spain's general governors always regarded us eventually made us enemies. Persecuted, walked on, degraded and broken, we divorced ourselves from our progenitors more and more and strived to defend our own vital interests, which no longer were compatible with Spain's.

Our bibliography, for example, was filled with more titles on slavery than any other subject. No other topic has drawn forth from our collective conscience better examples of self-sacrifice and solidarity. The antislavery message and its dissemination were almost entirely driven by Puerto Ricans. The names of Emeterio Betances, Segundo Ruiz Belvis, José Julián Acosta, Francisco Mariano Quiñones and Julio Vizcarrondo would have had free passage in our history by the mere act of presenting the safe-conduct of abolition. Reports lamenting how our black brethren suffered the shameful humiliation of being treated no better than animals shook the entire population for years.

The *Código Negro* (Negro Laws) gave sweeping powers to slave owners. Uprisings in Toa Baja, Bayamón, Vega Baja, Guayama and Ponce, though often punishable by death, by virtue of these laws, did not move the Puerto Rican spirit as much as the electrifying proclamations supported by abolitionist groups on the island and in Spain. Ever since the Spanish government promised special laws to govern the Antilles in 1837, which were never decreed,

Puerto Ricans included the immediate, definite and unconditional abolition of slavery as the first condition in every petition for administrative reform. The abolition of slavery was finally declared in 1873.

Naturally, along with the slaves' struggle for freedom, reformist sentiment began to grow, and conservatives deliberately connected it to the separatist movement. The fact was that abolitionists were the most ardent supporters of autonomy. The spirit of these men impregnated the moral climate and formed, little by little, the ideological atmosphere the people were to breathe until the end of the century.

I believe the first Puerto Rican who spoke valiantly and clearly about separatism was the dark poet, Daniel Rivera, author of the long poem *Agüeybana el Bravo*, published in a Ponce newspaper in 1854. His simple act of writing "Let he who was born in Spain, return to Spain" as a closing to the poem, expressed a desire to see "this pearl of the Iberian people free," and won him unrelenting persecution, forcing him to flee the country and finally die in exile. The Catalan Felipe Conde, who was publisher of *El Ponceño*, was fined 1,000 *pesos*. The court of first instance closed the newspaper down in due course and served to spark Luis Muñoz Rivera's publication, *La Democracia*. Such was the swift retaliation to our first cry for independence, spoken through an Indian cacique dead for more than 300 years, and daringly revived by a poet.

This Indian, who was the first to rebel against the conquistadores, became a symbol of liberation, and with defiant pride we conceitedly proclaimed ourselves the sons and daughters of the fierce Agüeybana. As war was being proclaimed on the Spaniards so were exclamations of Antillean solidarity. A proclamation circulated in 1864 regarding the transfer of the Puerto Rican Militia Battalion to the Dominican Republic begins, "Comrades: How long will we permit the despots of Spain to benefit from our inaction? A regiment of compliant militiamen from Puerto Rico has been taken by force to murder their counterparts in Santo Domingo. We have demonstrated our disaffection many times; many of our men are scattered in the mountains and some have hung themselves before consenting to go kill and rob our brothers." Remember the pasquinade written to Cortabarría, and the emotional road traveled is evident. The militiamen who so often offered their lives in defense of Puerto Rico preferred to flee and kill themselves before taking up arms against a people they considered not unlike their own.

The proclamation goes on to say: "And if they bring us by force as they have done to others, let us cross over and side with our brothers in Santo Domingo. They will see us as a godsend and welcome us with open arms us as they have already done with other Puerto Rican militiamen who have deserted the Spanish army...The *jíbaros* of Puerto Rico, sons of the fierce Agüeybana, have not yet lost their self-respect. Like the courageous Dominicans they will know how to treat their executioners and show them that though we are easy to govern when we are treated justly, we will not suffer abuse with impunity."

These were the days of more trenchant proclamations, manifestos, pasquinades, anonymous warnings, proclamations and the surreptitious attack and defense. Proliferating during this period were secret societies, codes, ambiguous cheers, undecipherable metaphors, double-entendre toasts delivered at dances, baptisms, parties and birthdays; all these constituted the sole motives for public meetings. Very little material of this kind remains, making us, in effect, orphans of the best repository for these "treasonous" and highly important materials: the press.

Our people's lack of interest in its recorded life is clear. Along with the destructive collaboration of storms, we find periodic bonfires of public documents ignited by the government, mysterious fires in unsuccessful attempts on archives, the absence of town libraries, and official indifference to these valuable historical resources. Had our interests been different we could have easily uncovered the decalogue of our civic life penned by our best authors in newspaper columns that are lost to us through fraud and disinterest. I daresay without fear of equivocation that the best part of native, intellectual production is not in books, but on the pages of newspapers and magazines. It is in the press where the best concentration of our collective conscience is distilled. We are indebted to her for the formation of upright men and women of character who were our cornerstones in the nineteenth century. Puerto Rican literature in general lacks a patriotic subtext. With rare exceptions its subjects were human social problems. Its technique as well as its themes are foreign. On the other hand, the press did not shrink from complicated issues and perfectly recorded our misfortunes, effectively laying bare the soul of our culture.

During this period Puerto Rican journalism was born, experienced its pinnacle and provoked another chain of arbitrary acts and uneven matches. Capricious censorship, suppression of newspapers, wholesale accusations and incarcerations, systematic and abusive persecutions all began to wear down the friendly nexus that united us to Spain, making a definitive distinction between our heretofore common interests.

To think, feel and act as a Creole we had to hide. The countryside was covered with secret societies cradling regional aspirations behind closed doors in order to shut out accusers and their suspicions. When the history of Puerto Rico's Masons is written their visionary projects and resolutions, nurtured in the shadows, to treat civic problems will be flooded by patriotic light. In this luminous cavern the Lares rebellion of 1868 was conceived. Despite the aborted plan (due to lack of synchronization and a haphazard beginning), it left in our loving care the memory of those national heroes who lost their lives in a gesture that could not fully succeed. Nevertheless *El Grito de Lares* (the Lares Call to Arms) was the shot in the arm that restored the health of our national patriotism.

The consequences, however, were fatal. The government more than quadrupled the number of witch hunts; more and more we were corralled by an army of suspicions, propped up by allegations and slander. Puerto Ricans began to lose their miserable little jobs and even native business and commerce suffered losses in a bloodless but merciless civil war. The country, which had already become a people, did not surrender easily and, "out of desperation," wrote José C. Barbosa, "organized a vast secret society as a last resort, officially called *La Torre del Viejo* (The Old Man's Tower), for the aid, protection, defense and progress of Puerto Ricans, which the people sanctioned by renaming it *Los Secos y Mojados* (The Dry and Wet). Only Puerto Ricans could belong to this society."

Their fates were sealed: Spaniards on one side, Puerto Ricans on the other. At this time the term "unconditional Spaniards" takes on a harrowing significance beside the phrase "conditional Spaniards." The Dry and Wet Society was primarily organized for economic and social reasons in an effort to defend *boricua* interests. This defense of our people was directed toward aiding local commerce, protecting native sons, educating children, sheltering widows, creating *boricua* cooperatives, all through charitable organizations. "All members," states Dr. José C. Barbosa in an article, "are duty bound, under oath, not to undertake any transaction, buying, selling or business of any kind with a firm, store or company that does not employ Puerto Ricans or accept them as clerks."

Upon declaring this boycott, our collective sensibilities are forced by circumstance to establish again a clear difference between the "native son" and the "foreign born."

Puerto Ricans thrilled to this restorative aspiration. Blacks and whites, rich and poor, farmers and urbanites, workers and professionals, blue-collar and white-collar workers came together amicably under the shade of this new brotherhood. Its influence was quickly felt through the rapid growth of native commerce, industry and business.

Prosperity did not last long. The Old Man's Tower was persecuted. Denunciations gave the government opportunities to initiate a reign of terror characterized by barbaric and shameful inquisitional cruelty. Any Puerto Rican who has read the history of the infamous *Compontes*, started in 1887, will feel his blood boil with indignation, and his stomach turn at such unjust and inhuman abuses. Young and old alike were pistol-whipped by "peace" officers attempting to wrench confessions about what many were ignoring. The innocent were incarcerated, treated no better than criminals; respectable faces were insolently slapped; under a scorching sun defenseless persons pushed to the ground and tied elbow to elbow were tortured with lashings, canings, kicks and death threats by firing squad. Others had their fingers crushed with twine and small sticks, arms and bones dislocated or broken. Along with testicular twisting, other heinous torments and mutilations were committed, such as being tied to the back of a horse, which might have been defensible if not for the sheer injustice and bloodthirsty grimaces with which they were carried out. This quagmire of innocent blood, derogatory insults and rabid contempt is what is historically known and dramatically labeled *Compontes.*

Autonomists, conveniently linked to The Dry and Wet Society, were also persecuted for attempted crimes, disobedience, sedition and secret conspiracies. Not only did humble day workers and poor farmers suffer the ire of the police and military courts, so did our most outstanding public-spirited patriots, among whom was a seminal figure of our culture, Román Baldorioty de Castro, and the Spaniard Laureano Cepeda, editor of a bold Ponce newspaper.

Contrary to public opinion, these historical events were of greater importance to the country than the *Grito de Lares.* The entire island was of one mind. Many towns, including Ponce, Juana Díaz, Mayagüez, Yauco and Guayanilla, substantially enriched their histories through the firm resolve with which they faced Spanish panic. Against all odds, a secret commission from Ponce was able to reach Madrid where other Puerto Ricans awaited them in order to place the disgraceful case of Puerto Rico before the Spanish government. It resulted in the fulminating dismissal of the governor general, Romualdo Palacio. This triumph, so well earned by our collective efforts, sustained for many years the optimism of those who gave the best years of their youth to shaping it.

Attempts to organize were always thwarted by official blows. The same hand that assailed the Civilian Institute prevented the opening of the Central Grammar School and delayed the founding of the *Ateneo* for over a quarter of a century, and also destroyed any hope of founding a university. In Pezuela's time, a three-person protest was branded seditious. Imprisonment without cause, suspension of civil rights, arbitrary orders, abuses, accusations and other outrages disbanded us without fully achieving the creation of the myth called public opinion. Yet when we were able to form Puerto Rican fellowship, our disjunctive individualism always impeded cohesion, splintering us into small groups with no force or backbone. Remember what became of the Autonomist Party, the Federal Party, the Puerto Rican Union and Alliance? Let us all honestly sing a *mea culpa*.

But our dreams to form a hardworking, dignified people cannot be in vain. We have paid too heavy a price for them throughout our history; in them is found our most heartfelt desire to be first and foremost Puerto Rican. Through the course of our common misfortunes a homeland culture painfully took shape. The worthiest propositions for our affirmation were filtered through religious, educational, political, economic, artistic and social layers. And this is what interests us at the moment. According to Spengler, "Culture is that union of the soul's expression in word and deed...a historical drama, [our] image within the image of universal history, the union of great sentimental and intellectual symbols, the only language through which a soul can express how it endures."

New suffering is inflicted upon our social body beginning in 1898. Its polemical proximity compels us for the moment to evade it. Let us instead look now for the roots of Puerto Rican-ness in the uniqueness of our own expression.

Roots

We've been on a long distance flight providing a bird's-eye view of parts of the historical landscape upon which Puerto Rican affirmation is grounded. In this section we intend to penetrate the secret dominions of totalitarian life. It is not enough to note the external workings of events; we must look at the hidden spectacle within the collective soul. Let's climb down from the tree-tops to study roots and osmosis at work; both explain our character and give it meaning.

In due course, the man that was shaped here gradually began differentiating himself from the original predecessors. The Creoles, products of the land, slowly but surely manifested preferences and tastes, attaining ways the Spaniards branded as displays of autonomous leanings. It is neither convenient nor necessary to point out the best examples of Puerto Rican expression, since we can discover their dissemination even in the most basic manifestations of daily life.

Reflecting upon the unbridled enthusiasm our people have for equine sports, I've often asked myself if this 100 year-old passion might perhaps be one of the distinctive marks of our psychological makeup. More than a tendency toward games of chance or a predisposition to the nervous excitement of betting and the hope of resolving our personal problems in one Sunday afternoon, there are historical factors behind this sport that serve to explain our state of mind. The *jíbaro*, central figure in our culture, seems to be a man sewn to his horse, a witness forever mute about his physical toil, diversions and passions. When reviewing the sparse collection of newspapers published in the past century, one often comes across accounts describing missing horses. These extensive advertisements do not exclude the minutest detail and some sound like lamentations at the loss of a loved one. In all of Puerto Rico's fairs and exhibitions our horses were always represented since they were the main attraction. Unfailingly they were the most important specimens in the animal husbandry section. In the much acclaimed Ponce exhibition of 1882, forty-six of the fifty-one animals presented were horses. These won awards for physical condition and appearance, height, single foot, walk, lope, trot, piaffe and gallop. Prizes were also awarded for harnesses, riding gear and saddles. During the exhibition of 1855 a horse of the finest European or African lineage was offered as a prize "to the owner of the best horse ranch."

Horse and cattle ranching was one of the most flourishing industries in Puerto Rico for many years. The industry's success was guaranteed by a fascination for three things: power, comfort and luxury. "Since time immemorial," writes José G. del Valle in 1896, "horse races have been held in Puerto Rico, and the island's inhabitants show great enthusiasm and skill for the sport." This enthusiasm led Puerto Ricans to baptize a genre of folk songs and even a dance with the name "*cabayo*," close in spelling to *caballo* (horse). For a time it was extremely popular. Even today, when considering the merits of a person we say he or she is "a hell of a colt."

In the year 1849, it occurred to Governor Juan de la Pezuela to prohibit the San Juan and San Pedro races. Opposition was unanimous. The people protested with every means at their disposal, even at the *Plaza de Armas* in our capital city where a small earthen jar was found with a note sticking out of it that read: "Open me before I burst/ inside is found Pezuela's bust."

When the jar was opened a folded sheet of paper was found containing enraged verses dressing down the governor; it was richly deserved. The governor had capriciously canceled one of the more emotional, time-honored events of the island. The prohibition was short-lived. Where does such an expensive avocation come from? Why does it even produce the following popular rhyme?

> My wife and my horse
> died at the same time.
> To hell with the wife;
> it's my horse I miss most!

During the first period of our history and in the beginnings of the second, Puerto Rico's population was dispersed in a geographical area characterized by marshes, gullies, rivers, few roads and the distances between houses. The need for a simple means of communication gave us no other recourse than to depend on the horse, an animal we mastered to the great surprise of Spaniards and foreigners alike. Not only men, but women also distinguished themselves by their riding expertise, which according to Friar Iñigo, "they executed with extraordinary ease." Years later the French traveler Pierre Ledru will make the same observation: "I doubt our fair Frenchwomen could take on the art of handling a horse with as much grace and daring as the amazons of Puerto Rico." Pedro Tomás de Córdova, the first historian to emerge in the nineteenth century, also affirms that "the neighbors' favorite diversions are dancing, horse races and cock fights. The ladies ride with much grace and are excellent horsewomen."

In these simple peculiarities reflecting our spirit a distinctive and original way of performing an activity so common to all peoples is evident, a way so particular and unique it clearly expresses an affirmation of our own personality. All the countries in the world ride horses. Nonetheless Puerto Ricans doing the same thing before the eyes of European observers convert the act of mounting and riding a horse into something so distinctive that we are able to clearly discover a pure expression of the national soul and an innate proclivity. This rhythm and proclivity begin to become something very much our own, differentiating itself from the rhythm and proclivity of the Spanish conscience, so inseparable at other times.

Horse races, with their diverse kinds of lariats and halter rings, were a must at formal occasions and popular festivals. In them the locals distinguished themselves with singular and inimitable grace. "Notwithstanding the throngs and confusion of the races," Iñigo Abbad states, "an accident rarely occurs, and in the off chance it does, it is to some Spaniard, who finding himself turning a corner before a squad of riders does not know how to avoid the encounter with the dexterity of the Creoles." The dexterity of the Creoles! This dexterity, so quietly hidden in the pages of history, is evidence of the inchoate ethnic autonomy that starts to define us.

Newer means of communication and recreation are slowly reducing old equine obsessions but, despite its curtailment, it is still so representative of who we are. Our preoccupation with horses has declined greatly and the animal has almost been relegated to sugar plantations and the race track. Although the track promotes raising the animals, the country's horses continue to be imported. So, are the observations we just made responsible for the unbridled enthusiasm our people have always felt for the sport? Let us continue on foot now, and next seek our image in dance and music.

In the *Almanaque de las Damas* (Ladies' Almanac of 1887), another European writer, Manuel Fernández Juncos, notices the rhythmic and delicate way Puerto Ricans walk, ultimately comparing it to our regional dances. "They walk with the same elegance," he says, "the same easygoing, semifluid flexibility, and to a certain beat no one else hears, but that reminds one of the musical weeping in 'La Borinqueña' and the playful turns of 'Sí, José.'" One of our popular folk songs embraces the same thought:

> You walk so gracefully
> that when I see you pass
> at times I imagine
> the street wants to dance.

The cultures of the world's diverse peoples have placed the rich content of their rhythms in their gait and dance. In the dance, as in art and poetry, the distinctive notes of a people's collective character are eloquently presented for all to see. "Although dance be universal," states Federico de Orís, "all peoples have their way of

dancing and their dances constitute one of the most characteristic and inimitable expressions of the national soul."

Learning how to dance was no easy feat in a stretch of land as small as ours. What Puerto Rican is not moved at the sound of the galvanic music of our *seis chorreao*? The *seis*, the *mariyandá* and later the *plena*, accompanied by other Antillean forms, required the organization of a native orchestra in which the three racial elements at our core come into play. The indigenous people offered the *cacharro* or *güiro* and the *maracas*. Africans transformed the indigenous tambourine and offered the *bomba* and the *bongó*. Spaniards gave us their guitar, which we have not altered but transformed into our guitars: *tiple*, *bordonúa* and *cuatro*, each born on our soil. With these instruments (Creole products with the exception of the guitar), we created our high-spirited *música brava*. But our climate is not conducive to such repeated excitement and our temperament, importing and assimilating cadences from other lands, found more reserved and soothing expressive forms and made way for the *danza*. So is completed both sides of one coin. Our high-spirited music, *música brava*, is joyful, propulsive, giddy; the *danza* is sad, soft, tranquil. The *danza* is to us what the fox-trot is to North Americans. A sports-oriented country on the move and strong, North Americans needed choreographed exercises consonant with their athletic constitution. On the other hand, Puerto Rico, an anemic tropical country, looked to couch its expression in a slow and modest dancing formula with beginning steps we call *paseos* and interludes that permit cordial dialogue. Our *danza*, unlike the fox-trot, invites joviality and conversation. Its waning movements with intermediate pauses are restful, comfortable and attuned to the climate's demands. It serves as a respite from our *música brava*.

Like other factors contributing to our uniqueness, the *danza*'s elements, as we have already stated, are not purely autochthonous. They were derived from other lands and surrendered themselves to our tastes, and after a process of spiritual metabolism emerged transformed and equal to our interior rhythms. We poured untold facets of our personality into the *danza*, producing one of our most

authentic cultural figures by virtue of his plain words and interpretation, namely, Juan Morel Campos. His genius, rich in *boricua*
material, has not been equaled in the history of our music. As
exquisite as their talents are, Tavárez and Quintón trail behind him.
Morel Campos adds to his prolific talent the collective sentiments
of an entire nation. His *danzas*, so personal and autobiographical,
can synthesize the doleful dialogue in our homeland very
well. "Sopapos" (Slaps), "No me toques" (Don't Touch Me), "Ten
piedad" (Have a Heart), "Vano empeño" (Desire in Vain), "Mis
penas" (My Troubles), "Tormento" (Torment) are titles reflecting
the drama common to us all. "Un diálogo" and "Conversación"
define the *danza*.

The realms of music and poetry are to be commended for
gathering the most hidden heartbeats within a nation's breast.
Neither in Europe nor in the Americas have I heard a fox-trot inter-
preted as aptly and authentically as by any run-of-the-mill musician
in the United States. In order for the Argentinean tango, Cuban
danzón, Colombian *bambuco* or Venezuelan *joropo* to be inter-
preted faithfully it is necessary that the interpreter be completely
saturated in the territorial spirit from where the pieces emanate.
With regard to our *danza* the difficulty is a notch higher. Have the
finest foreign musician play the *danza* and his failure is instantly
obvious. Just as with Spanish flamenco, some intangibles that don't
appear on the music sheet must be played: unwritten peculiarities,
indefinable and fleeting that cannot be pretended, and are privy
only to the native.

Our *danza* has often been called a piece of musical folly. More
than annoy us, the remark should make us protect our joy all the
more. I find in this "folly" the most visible affirmation of who we
are. In the three against two count note, that elastic triplet evenly
accented and that mathematically equals the other two notes, a
unique aspect of who we really are is contained.

The *danza*, like our landscape, is feminine, mild and romantic.
Due to its invariability of rhythms with limited registers, tiresome
repetition, overly sentimental tonality, its poor accompaniment—
and above all due to the lack of an inspired musician who will treat

it the way Chopin treats the music of Poland, and Albéniz the music of Spain—the *danza* has not been able to reach the critical plane of pure art. It lacks artistic idealization, refinement and ample registers necessary to enter a concert hall. Even here the *danza* is a faithful reflection of what and who we are. Our culture cannot yet aspire to a comfortable position in an international competition.

The fact that the *danza* did not finish developing should not prohibit it from being seen as a means to redeem the island. If we proceed to analyze its structure we will see how the *danza* is better served by rejecting the very common, hackneyed binary form and bolster itself on four parts and a prologue that can serve as the introduction. Of the former the most important and expressive is the third, climax of all *danzas*, which corresponds to lombardino's obbligato; it is the most heartfelt and nationalistic of the four, and does not cowardly entrust itself to foreigners nor sol-fa virtuosos.

Because we have not had a grand and glorious history, or a small epopee, a *danza* is our substitute for the national anthem we have yet to create. Simple souls with good intentions have convened assemblies of our musicians at various times to select an anthem. No selection has ever been sanctioned by the people. National anthems emerge under other augurs, without state flowers or juries. The people, with keener political insight, have preferred to sanction with their vote a descriptive, danceable *danza* with bourgeois rhetoric. "La Borinqueña" offends no one and is a native-born daughter of our patriotism. As a *danza* it is a legitimate daughter of the culture. And for now, it will have to do.

So there is, indeed, a Puerto Rican way of behaving. It is the foreigner, with better means of comparison than the locals, who has clearly observed it. The Venezuelan R. M. Carabaño writes in an essay the following warning: "Though the writer is a foreigner [a Puerto Rican] he has made an effort to ensure that both theater pieces have a totally regional flavor and color, making his characters speak and behave as genuine Puerto Ricans." Señor Carabaño observed not only that there is a way of comportment but also a way of speaking that is uniquely our own.

In mounting a horse, in walking, in dancing, in behavior, in speech, we begin to discover unique ways that define us. As a student at Columbia University in New York, I met many Latin Americans who would often point out characteristics peculiar to us. I would amuse myself listening to the accent and turns of expression of a Colombian classmate, and I had not noticed he was just as amused listening to me. He seemed to sing with that musical inflection that Mexicans, Venezuelans and Argentineans each have in their own way. One day, once we felt at ease with each other, he said, "You have such a charming way of speaking." Right away I responded, "Why, I thought you were the one who had a charming way of talking." When he explained what this "charming" way of speaking consisted of, mimicking my accent and imitating my intonation, which he found common to other compatriots of mine, I realized that we too have a particular inflection exclusively our own and original. Indeed every people carries the soul of their race and regional spirit in their mother tongues. Puerto Rico also adds its note to the rich pentatonic scale of the Spanish language.

We cannot characterize with exactitude our intonation. However, it is easy to hear that our speaking tone is sharper than that of Castilian Spanish. This higher frequency of tone makes ascending inflections lower than Spain's and interrogative sentences not notably different than declarative sentences. Isn't this just like our lives? This melodic disregard is made abundantly clear in the monotony of our school lectures. Our questions, which generally rise in intonation, fall toward the end in a supplicating tone. This may be rooted in our fatalism.

Language is the vault in which the embodiment of a people is deposited. Against the continuous, rhythmic pounding of days it begins to store words, turns of expression and maxims full of heroic postures confronting life out of spiritual necessity. In times of sweeping change, circumstantial words that at a given moment in history completed their ephemeral mission are lost. Others filled with philosophical meaning permanently take their places guarding, as though they were sacred coffers, the color, tone and differentiating character of the people that created them. Our nation did not build a language, but knew how to make its mark upon the backbone of the language it had inherited. Just as all other Latin American nations we also possess shades of differences that do not originate from importations but are rooted in our soil's temperament, spontaneously saturated with the typical traits of our personality.

Orthographically we offer no differences at all, but from the orthoepic point of view, the Spanish language as spoken in Puerto Rico joins its interesting peculiarities to those distinguishing other regions of America from Spain. Among ourselves we find the very common phenomenon of phonetic localism that in many countries is often defended by the alliance formed between regionalism and carelessness. Needless to say correct pronunciation of a language is not completely uniform in any country in the world.

Though the best wishes of this author are in favor of a less adulterated pronunciation tending toward a greater consolidation of the spoken language, I cannot help but point out those peculiarities that circulate in our provincial orthoepy. The most popular are pronouncing the Spanish *ll* like *y*, and *z* and *c* before *e* and *i* as an *s*. Excessive nasality for vowels in contact with consonants as in *cantan*, *ñape*; aspiration of the final syllabic *s*, lifting the tongue toward the soft palate on the final *n* of a word, aspiration of *j*, the uvular *rr*, and among the cultured a legitimate, though misguided desire to pronounce several silent letters such as *p* in *séptimo* and *septiembre*; *b* in *obscuro*, *substituto*; pronouncing the *cc* in *lección* and *acción* like *ks* instead of *gs*, which is correct; pronouncing the final *m* in *álbum* and *item*, which should be pronounced like an *n*. These idiosyncracies and phonetic defects cradled in our "charming" intonation are characteristically Puerto Rican.

Long before the majority of South American republics, we were able to complete our own *Diccionario de Provincialismos* (Dictionary of Regional Expressions), which is an excellent reference work on the Puerto Rican contribution to the Spanish language. (We owe a debt of gratitude to Augusto Malaret, author of said work and the best *Diccionario de Americanismos* published to date). All of this attests to the distinct way Puerto Ricans speak, just as there is a way of thinking distinctly Puerto Rican.

We are deeply preoccupied with being correct and it is

poignant to hear radio announcers who, in their eagerness to pronounce their *c*'s and *z*'s, place them in words that require an *s*. The
uninformed usually smile when hearing the numerous obsolete
words commonly used by our *jíbaros*, believing them to be vulgar,
plebeian and incorrect. The terms *truje* (I brought), *jablar* (to
speak), *lamber* (to lick), *mesmo* (the same), *dende* (where), *dotor*
(doctor) and so many others used in the most outstanding classics
of Spain's *Siglo de Oro* (Golden Age of Literature) is perfect
Castilian Spanish, held in reserve since the sixteenth century in the
mouths of our farmers, offering for our contemporary interest a
precious phenomenon suspended in time. However, this fact, commonplace in some Latin American countries, does not allow for any
claims on the culmination of *jíbaro* speech. Along with these old
words of fine vintage stock our rural folks created others such as
atrecho (shortcut), *avancino* (presumptuously familiar or meddle-
some), *cumblera* (the two-sloped roof of rural homes and other
edifices reminiscent of the *bohío*), *cucubano* (firefly), *ñangotarse* (to
crouch down), *pollona* (a female chicken not yet a hen), *malojillo*
(wheat-colored grasses for livestock). All have been in circulation
for over a hundred years.

Add to this battle an obsession with linguistic purity, region-
alisms, archaic language and neologisms, plus our current status as
bilinguals, which demands our utmost linguistic attention, and our
preoccupation with ultracorrect form in language is understand-
able. According to the prominent philologist Navarro Tomás, it is a
defense mechanism so as never to be caught in a careless error. In
the written word and above all in public speaking a servile propensity to Gongorist, pompous embellishment is notable as we have
already explained in discussing our rhetoricalness. In that chapter
we also pointed out the cause of our meandering speech, as exuber-
ant as it is slippery.

The metaphor is the one door open to our dreams of liberty.
The language of the student, the peasant and the masses is a marvelous inheritance of metaphors. Trades, cockfighting, horse racing
and politics are ovens for permanent metaphorical baking. So it
should be with a people whose own metaphor, *par excellence*, is its

own life. More than living it candidly, we suggest it, skirting around it, listening attentively to the outsider's voice and to our fantasies. We know how to accommodate and adapt to circumstances. Skill in skirting an issue has contributed greatly to our propensity for assimilation.

"There's nothing like a new problem to distract you from an old one," we were told once by Hispanic optimism. But our very core, assaulted by physical and man-made phenomena, and filled with uneasiness and skepticism, vented the insistent sense of this maxim by putting the expression back into circulation as a Puerto Rican lament: "A new problem can indeed drive out an old one, if they don't both persist." The ability for both to remain is a testament to our distrust, commonly taking the shape of the ever so popular *nju* (uh-huh). Recourse to such malapropisms have also served to openly express *boricua* sentiments.

On this topic one can go on and on, but in view of the brief treatment given other topics in these essays, we must abandon it for now. Add to the guardedness of our metaphorical lives the elucidating customs covered in the previous chapters and one will possess, with some exactitude, a provisional set of behaviors operating uneasily in our collective unconscious.

These days when we analyze Puerto Rican endocrinology, we immediately notice that some hormones have lost their old energetic cathexis and others are found in an altered state. Some examples have practically disappeared such as folkloric and religious festivals; horse racing has become limited to commercial events. A losing battle is being waged over preserving traditions we hold dear like patriarchal customs and Christmas festivities. In the end all share the old-fashioned isolation of the past, offering for our contemplation the spectacle of the dichotomies in dispute: Catholicism and Protestantism, the fox-trot and the *danza*, English and Spanish, The Three Kings and Santa Claus, the party and the *parranda*, in sum, Europe and the United States.

The oxidation process is obvious, and in some cases necessary and useful. While this transmutation of what we are takes place, it is venturesome to ascribe definitive behaviors in our changing personality. To describe our character—when the indecisiveness of these years is over—future generations will need to remember the promiscuity of current times.

A country like ours, which began to delineate its own sense of self within Hispanic culture, cannot consider itself vanquished or worn out. We must have faith in those latencies. We have an unmistakable way of being but these ways, which never experienced the joy of developing fully, today find themselves damaged by the transformation inflicted upon it by a new culture's alchemizing process.

Let us pull out dry lifeless roots and nourish only those that contain hearty plant lineages. By the same token why travel unclothed when there is apparel in our luggage? Even if we dispose of what is out of date, there is still more than enough to wear. In this hour of transitory doubt we need to delve into all those things that connect our introverted natures. No *responsos*; no *glorias in excelsis*. At least some serious meditation to increase the light of Puerto Rico's star.

Our Most Precious Treasure: The Young

the time has come to take our leave of the reader so that he may proceed alone on his pilgrimage toward the homeland. We are at the last stop in the book and saying farewell is unavoidable. While en route the reader would have been able to see that to the left and right of us there were streets we should have passed through. In addition the reader would have recognized stops already visited on his own or with a guide, and even deemed some so unnoteworthy they should have been bypassed altogether. This essay does not caress or remain indifferent, does not intend to outrage, nor was it meant to be dogmatic; it is rather a debate written with fidelity to the facts, without attenuations, but without indifference, and its hope is to incite Puerto Rican youth to reconstruct the subject proposed here with new ingredients.

I invite those able to piece together a graphic account of Puerto Rican customs to find the fingerprints of our collective soul and make them clearer and better defined. This will entail an openness to admitting our sins and defects so as to prepare for the long roster of duties ahead with a firm resolve to reform. To do this we must stifle the personal ambitions that turn our country into a hostel. Instead, we must push ahead with a squadron of honorable convictions impervious to tempting offers.

In the last eight to ten years an awakening has occurred in our young people that although sporadic is responsible for attitudes auguring a new budding consciousness. Place all your faith and hope in that renewed body of young men and women. Already this germinating, future flower is a revelation that men of my generation ought to encourage. Clearly today's youth, whom I stand behind, have problems worthy of our attention. Instead of looking at my generation's problems, let us first consider those of the present, still dumbstruck by the din from two contradictory coasts.

Today's youth has walked through a gorge formed, to date, by disillusionment and enticement. To one side is the Spanish culture that speaks to our emotions, to the other is the United States addressing our intellect. Both compel us to move our heads from one side to the other, listening to solicitations made to us at the same time. Our generation was caught in the fire between these two and has been passively sustaining itself from memories and promises, nostalgia and foreboding, from achievements and hopes, without ever clarifying the unknowns of its present situation.

We are a frontier generation, ground down by an ending and a new beginning, not knowing where to address the necessary requisitions so as to assume our own responsibilities. As the twentieth century began, we were already abandoned by our historical mother, and remained in the care of a rich and enterprising stepfather. A whirlwind of decisions has kept us indecisive in the high seas of distrust, waiting to hear at any moment "every man for himself."

Despite the alteration of old cultural molds by the displacing effects of the Spanish American War, Puerto Ricans defrayed the difficult cost of these times with a series of their own characteristics, credits indicating the people's spiritual survival. Ours are a good number of sacrifices that now ought to form the foundation of our true nature. But today's polemical attitude keeps yesterday's traits and today's, which are in our best interest to connect, hidden from us.

There are those who would like the past to turn into dust; others who strive to maintain it intact, as if it were an irreplaceable rock, without considering the parts we have prevailed over and the parts that are decayed. We have been so attentive to the Spanish and American dimension, we have forgotten to seek the third dimension, our own. The Puerto Rican dimension is the only one that compels us to select and order those things from today and the past that it suits us to keep for the future. When we handle both cultures we cannot, nor should we, turn our backs on the naturalized lineages that shape the outline of our character. Spengler has stated, "History consists of current events driving toward the future but with a rear view to the past." We must answer this call with daily endeavors, not deferentially, but giving an entirely Puerto Rican sense to the future. Throw your support behind the vanguard because we live in a time of unforeseeable possibilities and are not tending to the cultivation of our fundamental interests.

Returning to the past is futile. The spirit's fickleness does not suffer backsliding. It constantly shakes off any ashes from the past without removing the live coals in whose embers today's bread begins to brown. We need not defend less-than-perfect intentions from the transformations needed. Every epoch has its rearrangement of priorities and poses questions that can only be responded to with new creations from the new culture. Besides the systems of government, the eras that today are at war are radically and necessarily distinct. We cannot remove ourselves from world changes that at given moments have fatefully pressed their hands upon our shoulders.

If returning to the past is impossible, it is in every respect in vain to go forward denying our heritage and, what's worse, being ignorant of the historical alluvium that has flowed from the finest tributaries of this country. Before assigning ourselves future tasks, we must research the past to ascertain what skills we can count on to achieve them. As today's youth moves about within a seeming functional laxity, they appear to be a generation of invalids unable to weigh this reality with any precision. Today's young men and women cannot find the shortest path to rediscover Puerto Rico. They face a pessimism rooted in past disillusionments and today's failures, an optimism rooted in past advantages and current complacencies, both within a resentful rancor toward outsiders that is favorably disposed to obey and adapt. Young people delegate too much, and some responsibilities cannot be passed on to others. They are becoming spoiled by the acrimonious ferment of the two nations that wall them in, and neglect to fill the content of our character with their own traits.

If we cannot as yet declare that our Spanish heritage finds itself bankrupt, we can at least affirm that the business of the spirit has suspended payments altogether. See it from the angle of public decorum and it becomes apparent that the moral panorama has narrowed, making the ineffable pathways to our soul difficult to see. Puerto Ricans in 1898 were stunned at the change from one empire to another, losing sight of the balance essential to create new reasons to dream. This is why a new generation of meagerly endowed youngsters emerged who have had to disconcertedly sort through states of abandonment and experimentation, estrangement and rapprochement, ambition versus achievement.

The men and women of my generation have looked in vain for someone with intestinal fortitude superior to ours, in whose uncorrupt and protective shade we could clearly hear the voice of our myth. Frequently when political avarice blindly throws a ball our way, this generation dubiously looks upward at the void, which should have been filled with the like of Hostos, Giner, Rodó, Varona, shapers of nations and consciences. To what youth-oriented confessor have we been able to raise the issues of young people sowing wild oats, or the problems afflicting each one in the decisive moments where the intervention of an understanding, edifying and loyal counselor with their own inspiring light would have helped? Who can we hold up as an example when the need to interpret life presses us to fully understand the sumptuary aspects of existence, so inevitable if one wants to respond nobly to the questions of each historic moment? Where shall we find the earnest hand that pushes at the right time and at the right time holds back the impulses of youth, so needful of the evangelistic benevolence of a teacher?

A teacher! In public life we have had various approximations rendered useless to serve the public by one or another alienating faction. Along with this wonderful divisiveness we have also concocted a group of contingent leaders. I don't think anyone is going to confuse a leader of the people with an impresario of public opinion. Political and social climbing upstarts remain in last place and are a plague of locusts on the budget, draining it of any cultural content or a facsimile thereof. All want to serve, but few truly do so.

To expect more courageous contributions from our young people it is necessary to first come up with a new means of appraising men and women. We must rescue dignity and decency from the street in order to restore their pristine sense. We have to turn out that spurious thing some have taken to calling patriotism and that is passed around like a hired call girl. It is imperative that we make enemies of these shameless men that deprave the passions and pimp our youth by their example.

Society's scorn for public streetwalkers makes no sense when, on the other hand, they hold certain men in public life in high esteem. If in defense of public morals so-called common women are condemned, there is no reason not to also condemn common men. Prostitution, which shames society so, is not an exclusively female occupation. In our country morals are very flexible when it comes to concealing the corruption of those who should be the best guardians of a code of ethics.

Everywhere you go one hears, "This is unspeakable." Yet it is speakable and has a Christian name, but belongs to no denomination. During this historical transition when it is incumbent upon us to push ahead the second best, forming a chorus, if not stairs, so that these youngsters may move upward, we have been unable to see that we are forming beasts of burden out of a flock of masqueraders with no vote, no voice, no dignity. We do not have to be altar boys at all, but as long as we hold on to the censer we will be unable to occupy our hands with nobler duties.

These tamed youngsters should not allow the circumstances of the moment to break their spirit. Having the forbearance of a donkey is good, but not the donkey's docility for being mounted. To labor on behalf of obsequious youngsters is to leave ahead of us an empty space eagerly awaiting its men and women; and to fully become men and women they must first accrue merits through hard work and determination.

The greatest misfortune to befall our youth is their belief that they are nothing else and nothing more than that. Youth is not a vocation, not even an appropriate designation if you only reach it under false pretenses. It cannot hold any promise or hope as long as its inner sanctum is void of guiding revelations, disciplined efforts, and a charge of skilled energies, all at the service of good judgment. Youth should not pride itself in being a flower before it has performed those tasks that ripen its certainty of becoming a fruit. This conceit must be justified through prolonged efforts toward the fulfillment of one's duty. The kept promise is one of the most beautiful ways of keeping up to date with one's obligations. The new generation will not be able to assert its authority in the future, unless they abandon their insignificant trifles and commence using those cultivated aptitudes that enable them to draw from the inmost part of themselves.

The new generation is intellectually lazy, furthering the defeatism of a pernicious inferiority complex. Puerto Ricans are unable to strike a balance in their thought processes and are wont to fall in opposing poles when defining themselves. They either believe themselves inferior to the ape or the center of the universe. In the latter case, they move between pedantry and boastfulness, simulating by any means available the authority they lack. In the first case, they feel ground down and next to nothing, to such an extent that even their own essence is alien to them, and they come to believe their misery will never end.

It is up to today's young men and women to discard both attitudes at odds with our reality, and fill the chasm between these two fluctuating tendencies with equanimity. To arrive at the unassailable truth, being severe is preferable to being indulgent. Indulgence can never make peace between the excessive pretensions of the mediocre and the exemplary rigor of those who with their encyclopedic and comprehensive knowledge can afford to be importunate.

The crushing impact of today's inferiority complex can be

traced to geographical, historical and political limitations, favorable in any case for fusing self-contempt with a sense of insignificance. Needless to say, contempt is responsible for the circulation of that lot of stuffy, insufferably vulgar milquetoast, pinheads with small hearts who think and feel on a small scale.

The new generation of intermediators should note the pathological medium in whose shadow it forms itself. This is not a country of builders, but of ill-natured people. Everyone has an opinion, criticizes and destroys. Each is convinced of his expertise no matter if he falls short of the most basic qualifications. Everyone wants to be right, no one wants to lose. And because the dangers of secret thoughts, hidden agendas, deceitful intentions and sleights of hand have been a constant, when a new voice asks to speak he is insulted by those who wonder, "Now what does that character *really* want?" And instead of the new voice becoming uncontainable, it sticks in the craw until it chokes, and bright ideas become mildewed. So the field remains open for choruses, masquerades and the like.

Things will continue accordingly while this summering youth holds on tightly to its holiday. Critical discernment and firm resistance mean entering public life through a back door. Public service is a hardship and needs souls who will struggle unflinchingly, tenaciously, always face forward, never assuming a false front in combat or turning their backs in cowardly precaution.

Every day the press is awash in a sea of youth projects: manifestos, resolutions, regulations, courses of action, societies, premature groups that die at birth because they cannot realize themselves by themselves automatically as if by art of a miracle. This programmatic mania is ripping apart the planking of fledgling aspirations. Usually murdered by abulia, the project dies and youthful determination is lost, left by the riverside without ever having waded into the stream.

We must use integrity to remove this enveloping, contaminating attitude. Driven by a higher resolve, we must wipe out this blight of drives and projects, and in the arena of performance and execution, thrust and parry with hope as our sword. The last stroke is to demand from all of us, from every single one of us, the precise contribution that will convert every intention into a deed and every hope into a historical fact. If we do not faithfully keep our promises, the day will come when every abandoned idea and wasted opportunity or concept that never got beyond the project stage will rise up like ghosts to assault our middle-aged prudence and blow up in our faces with self-reproach and regret. But then it will be too late to start anew.

Young people with degrees should extend a fraternal hand toward blue-collar and civil service workers who need to share their troubles and expand their networks. We must be generous and open the tent of enthusiasm so that there may be room for all. As long as lost discouraged souls cannot be galvanized, and free-floating anxieties cannot be mortised in a comprehensive fusion of dreams, the mission of the young will remain unrecorded, leaving their elders to do badly what only they can do well: Inject sound health, new blood, optimism and joy in society's wasting body.

Liveliness and pluck, this is joy. The vigor of a people is provided in great measure by contentment, amusement and good humor, a sure sign of good health. During this gloomy Puerto Rican night it is her young who are called to turn on the lights of enthusiasm. I, of course, am not talking about that fragile joy that fades, but of the alluvium that reaches our soul as if it were a sacrament. There will be time enough for sadness when taxes begin to be paid, but these are the years consistent with sowing wild oats and dreaming young dreams. Sports should capture the interest of every young man who means to be so completely. But that cannot be enough. It must be accompanied by a joy in *mens sana* to avoid being reproached for bringing a harlot to their breast. Just as he must protect his happiness he also should take care of his seriousness of purpose, the only means of summoning himself before history and noticing his own breaches.

One of the seedbeds that should most preoccupy young people is the university. Every year the most distinguished students from our high schools fill its classrooms. They reach its very center and even graduate at the end of some years, still not knowing with any certainty the fundamental difference between one school and another. They are content to think the university is a step higher than high school and, what's worse, it starts a wild race for grades, a kind of persecutory, frenetic, reprehensible mania. The most depressing event in current university life is the ferocious preoccupation with those trinkets: A, B, C. To a certain point, professors and the Grade Point Index collaborate in converting a letter of the alphabet into the Holy Grail of culture. To no avail have I argued with colleagues on academic staffs about the flaws of measuring the efforts of each student with a system of grades that in the long run cannot be free of errors and capriciousness. An examination does not always indicate preparation, less so when it is given to prove what the student does not know. Obligatory class attendance is another requirement that will no longer be compulsory as soon as we become a true and authentic university. Our young men and women must address other fundamental problems that in some places affect the vital interests and concerns of qualified students, such as preparation and selection of professors; ranking, salaries and promotions; teachers' efficiency and service rendered outside as well as in the classroom; ability to make themselves understood and perfect their methods until they are able to make of the subject a medium for discussion, clarification and creativity; the elimination of matriculation fees that now exclude the needy, though they have talent; entrance limitations on the basis of class size; consideration of each faculty member's gifts and opinions; and fresh and positive ways for the university to reach the nerve center of the people.

I truly fear that our students lack the appropriate tools and are not up to the task of plummeting the depths of the intangible university. On the other hand, I am sure the student body expects from us, their own teachers, at the very least, a tiny handful of orienting ideas upon which to act on their own. But very few teachers dare to fish in deep waters for fear that the Dutchman may catch them.

In order for young men and women to cultivate the crystal clear principles that build character, teachers cannot be unopinionated entities, afraid of everyone including themselves. Rather than being talking textbooks or bogus guides, they must promote mental processes that help students carry out their duties eagerly. As long as guarantees regarding divergence of opinion do not exist in the university, it will never be more than a nursery school. If we all unselfishly shoulder the responsibility of our own ideas the university, in a short time, will be the most respected and prolific mother of the nation.

Nothing can be achieved if we remain on a Pablum diet. We must insist on frequency of service and strict fulfillment of duty.

I am not saying that young people should ignore politics, much less today when the fine art is exaggerated. No. Young men and women should not and cannot refrain from finding the lost beat of our drummer's struggles; their first duty is to synchronize that beat to the harmony of other interests that make up our people's composition. To influence the dominant ideas of political parties, they cannot approach them empty-handed, seeing them as meeting places where people gather merely to gossip. One should go to give, not receive, to show by example and with tolerance the serious convictions one holds, and not worsen the situation by participating in the dishonorable practice of discussing secrets openly. Young people's attitudes should smack of sacrifice and unnegotiable integrity so that their convictions will not be the result of private prearrangements. Honesty does not provoke distrust.

Once inside the core of social institutions, party affiliations must be put aside. There where science, art, religion, commerce, industry and duty are the unifying vertebrae, the young should break with party politics to assure that the credo of every institution is above all sectarianism. Politics should only take up a limited portion of every student's program and only if it does not overstep its boundaries since it can intrude upon and pry into even the most trivial details of every social function. When this is the case politics becomes the most deadly curse to befall a people.

Young people then must rid themselves of narcissism and enter everyday battles with new armaments. They should not disappear, however, at the first sign of trouble, but rather form the defenses necessary to wield the hammer of justice and straighten the twisted ideas that have declared war against the conscience.

To create, to believe—because in terms of faith we are weak

and with regard to creativity even worse. We have demonstrated ability for the technical manipulation of material and for consumption, but not production. Only he who has frequented life on a higher plane has the potential to create new values. We could point out deficiencies in literature, the press, ceramic arts and social activism. Still, let us look to music as an illustration.

The acute crisis of composers is quite odd because it affects the entire country. Within a framework of strict modernity we can count on notable performers, but there is not among them one alone that stands out as a composer, even a little. How unfortunate for Puerto Rico that among so many first-rate virtuosos of fine pedigree there is not a one that has distinguished himself as an author of musical pieces.

Virtuosity in art has a fleeting glory and although it offers the artist material benefits, it does not always resonate in the memory years later. The choicest and brightest examples of an art form often evaporate with the disappearance of the performer. The complex mechanisms that drive a virtuoso do not include the actual conditions propitious for standing the test of time, and ultimately the years diminish his powers. In the end the difference existing between a composer and a performer falls somewhere between an inventor and a mechanic with room to spare. The former is somewhat compelled to work anew, creating and conceiving, the latter depends on the first and is condemned to the transformable torment of repetition. Despite having its pleasures and offering variability he certainly walks over his own steps in an incessant return to the same thing.

Surely the young—the Sanromas, the Figueroas—put us on the international map of rhythm with their marvelous interpretations, both classical and modern; and surely other veteran spirits are also splendid supporters of musical art in Puerto Rico. Still, composers of our day, with very few exceptions, give no signs of life. In every respect and in a disproportionate way performance surpasses creation.

That our enervating and stale environment is primarily

responsible for this unproductive and sterile situation cannot be denied. Nonetheless now is the time to promote composition in every way possible and to pay tribute to artistic creation where and when it is merited, given that a good number of diverse academies are operating successfully, judging by the frequent auditions. Now that an activist institution, *Pro-Arte Musical,* exists since the Association of Musical Professors and the Symphonic Orchestra has made itself prominently known, and with the definitive support of the University of Puerto Rico, we can count on many virtuosos. There are never enough good musicians, but we do not have native composers, and we must forge them.

A series of themes are scattered in the air that clamor for musical interpretation. To know the soul of a cultured nation one has to refer to the poetry, painting and music of her people. Without this collaborative clarification, the prospects for her vitality become impossible to predict. Have our young contemporary virtuosos considered the prolific cooperation we all expect from them?

These pervaders of foreign music have prepared the way, and we are grateful. They shaped the environment, fine-tuning tastes, educating audiences and training the ear. Though this achievement has not reached its full measure, it is enough to encourage and generate the initiative needed in the future by our latent composers. We must assist this gestation with patriotism, generosity and with the honorable aspiration of filling this void in our homeland's culture as we speak.

We do not expect, nor desire, supplantations without benefit or advantage, but rather yearn for the same indispensable collaboration that exists in the theater between the author and the actors. Until now we have been content to exclusively consume music we have not produced. Let us continue to raise the volume of exquisite and imported music, but think always of helping to produce music native to our own country.

We must add to our condition of consumers that of producers. The time is ripe to incorporate Puerto Rico into the creative current of contemporary music. The same holds true for poetry, for the press, for everything. Create within ourselves in order to create the one whole.

The best way to create ourselves is to submit ourselves to the power of culture. Chance improvisation will prove risky before long because nations are not formed with merry thoughts and lavish concepts. These will turn into little more than a powder from the grinding mill of apprenticeship. Let us begin by dusting the powder off the past, dispersing the clouds over our horizon, and on it shall appear, for those who earn it and merit it, the star of Bethlehem.

Young women and men of my time, you might think that history begins now, that you are the ones called to fill its annals, to give it the ideal content any right-minded person would wish for their country. If you wish to be truthful with yourselves and truthful in answering the questions of the time in which we live, you must steer on all of history's highways and byways, and painstakingly make your mark so that one day your work will be recorded in posterity's annals. Otherwise you shall always remain chronologically young, never growing up, doomed to carrying your coffers empty.

Tend to the divine treasure within you because the highest degree can turn into little more than a series of letters after a name.

Glossary of Names

Abril, Mariano (1867-1935). Writer, politician and official island historian.

Acosta, José Julian (1825-1891). Distinguished journalist and editor of *El Progreso* a newspaper and primary voice of the Liberal Reformist Party.

Alonso, Manuel (1822-1899). Wrote *El Gíbaro* the first book that focused on Puerto Rican customs and daily life as a literary theme.

Baldorioty de Castro, Román (1822-1889). Considered the father of the Puerto Rican Autonomist Movement who also fought to abolish slavery and establish a constitution guaranteeing Puerto Ricans the same rights as Spaniards.

Barbosa, José Celso (1857-1921). A gifted medical doctor known as the father of the Puerto Rican statehood movement.

Balseiro, José A. (1900-?). Poet and novelist who wrote the critical work *El Vigía*.

Bécquer, Adolfo Gustavo (1836-1870). Spanish poet mostly known for the melancholic themes in his work.

Betances, Emeterio Ramón (1827-1898). Doctor who founded a hospital to save Puerto Ricans from a cholera epidemic. Also organized a clandestine society for the liberation of African slaves. Led the insurrection of El Grito de Lares.

Bibiana, Benítez María (1783-1873). The first woman poet to have her work, much of which emphasized historical themes, published in Puerto Rico.

Bourget, Paul (1852-1935). French writer of plays and novels.

Brau, Mario (1870-1941). Prominent water colorist and pen and ink artist.

Brau, Salvador (1842-1912). A historian, journalist, sociologist, novelist, and essayist. His books have made an important contribution to the study of boricua history, including *Historia de Puerto Rico and La colonización de Puerto Rico.*

Campeche, José (1752-1809). Son of a freed slave who became one of Puerto Rico's most eminent painters. He produced approximately 400 paintings and earned a reputation as "the most gifted of Latin American rococo artists."

Canales, Nemesio R. (1878-1923). Journalist, humorist, satirist and lawyer.

Castelar, Emilio (1832-1899). Writer, orator, and politician who became President of the first Spanish republic in 1873.

Castellanos, Juan de (1522-1607). Spanish writer who chronicled the conquest of Borinquén in the book *Elegía a la muerte de Juan Ponce de León.*

Cebollero, Pedro. Advisor to the Commissioner of Education. He wrote "A School Language Policy for Puerto Rico."

Cofresí, Roberto (1791-1825). Famous pirate who is part of the culture and lore of Puerto Rico.

Coll y Toste, Cayetano (1850-1930). Doctor, writer, poet and historian who wrote such works as *Puertorriqueños Ilustres and Prehistoria de Puerto Rico.*

Cordero, Rafael (1790-1868). A dedicated teacher who established elementary schools and taught the poorest children on the island for free.

Dávila, Virgilio (1869-1943). Poet and teacher. His works include: "Aromas del Terruño" and "Pueblito de Antes." Both reflect Puerto Rican traditions.

Diego, José De (1866-1921). A brilliant orator and a major poet known mostly for his advocacy of independence for Puerto Rico. Works such as "A Laura" and "Postuma" won him a lasting reputation as Puerto Rico' s finest love poet.

Fernández Juncos, Manuel (1846-1928). One of Puerto Rico's best known journalists, he launched the newspaper *El Buscapie* in 1876.

Figueroa, Jesús (1878-1971). Composed zarzuelas and danzas. He was the patriarch of the highly regarded musical family the Figueroas.

Ganivet, Ángel (1865-1898). Spanish novelist associated with the vanguard of the Generation of 1898 literary movement.

García Troche, Juan. One of the first Puerto Rican historians who co-wrote *Memoir and General Description of the Island of Puerto Rico* in 1582, the first account of the origins of Puerto Ricans.

Gautier Benítez, José (1848-1880). Considered the greatest poet of the romanticism period in Puerto Rico. His best known works are "Ausencia" and "Su Canto a Puerto Rico".

Gili Gaya, Samuel (1892-1976). Spanish philologist who wrote *Curso Superior de Sintaxis Española*.

Giner de los Ríos, Francisco (1839-1915). Spanish writer and philosopher that founded La Institución Libre de Enseñanza en Madrid.

Henríquez Ureña, Pedro (1884-1946). Essayist from The Dominican Republic who wrote noteworthy articles and books on the formation of Latin American culture.

Hostos, Eugenio María de (1839-1903). Played a major role in reorganizing the educational system of The Dominican Republic. His work *La Peregrinación de Bayoán* (1863) is a seminal work promoting Cuban independence and revealing through fiction the restrictions of the Spanish colonial regime.

Keyserling, Hermann Count (1880-1946). German writer and philosopher. Founder of the School of Wisdom.

Llorens Torres, Luis (1887-1945). Puerto Rican poet best known for his beautiful romantic works. His work is also renowned for its *criollismo*, an expression of nationalism.

López Landrón, Rafael. Puerto Rican who advocated against capital punishment in *Apuntes sobre la pena de muerte*, published in 1885.

Malaret, Augusto (1878-1967). Distinguished journalist and writer who studied Puerto Rican language usage that was accepted by the Real Academia Española.

Marañon, Gregorio (1887-1960). Respected Spanish writer, historian and physician.

Marín, Pachín (1863-1897). Journalist, poet and revolutionary that fought for the liberation of Cuba.

Mariano Quiñones, Francisco (1830-1903). Journalist, abolitionist leader, and founder of the newspaper *El Espejo* that disseminated autonomist ideology.

Matienzo Cintrón, Rosendo (1855-1913). Orator and politician, founder of the Liberal Reformist Party, and a leader in the struggle for Puerto Rican independence.

Matos Bernier, Félix. Cabinet member in the first autonomist government. He later founded the Federal Party, which favored annexation with the United States.

Meléndez Muñoz, Miguel. Writer, essayist and playwright of *Cuentos de la carretera central* and *Retablo puertorriqueño*.

Menéndez y Pelayo, Marcelino (1856-1912). Poet, historian and literary critic.

Morel Campos, Juan (1857-1896). The most important figure in Puerto Rican music of the nineteenth century, known primarily for his composition of danzas.

Muñoz Rivera, Luis (1859-1916). Journalist and political leader in the campaign for independence from Spain. He also served as resident commissioner in Washington, D.C.

Oller, Francisco (1833-1917). Considered the first Latin American impressionist, he adapted their obsession with light and color to brilliantly capture the island's local flora.

Ortega y Gasset, José (1883-1955). Spanish essayist and philosopher, writer of *La rebelión de las masas*.

Padilla Gualberto, José (1829-1896). Satirist, lyricist and poet. His work is compiled in "En el combate" and "Horas de pasión." He was also known as "El Caribe."

Padín, José. Commissioner of the Department of Education in Puerto Rico from 1932-1937.

Palés Matos, Luis (1898-1959). One of the creators of Afro-Antillean poetry, which introduced African rhythms and words into the idioms of Puerto Rican poetry in such works as *Tuntún de Pasa y Grifería* and *Últimos Poemas*.

Pfandl, Ludwig (1881-1942). Critic and writer who translated *Cultura y costumbres del pueblo español de los siglos XVI y XVII* from German to Spanish.

Picón Salas, Mariano (1901-1965). Venezuelan historian, essayist, and critic who expounded on the problems posed by Latin American culture.

Power, Ramón (1775-1813). In 1810 was elected and became the first Puerto Rican delegate sent to the Spanish parliament.

Quintón José, Ignacio (1881-1925). Composer and musician who performed danzas, a Puerto Rican musical genre.

Ribera Chevremont, Evaristo (1896-1976). Latin American modernist poet.

Rodó, José Enrique (1872-1917). Uruguayan writer and essayist who wrote "Ariel" in which he calls upon Latin America to hold cultural values that are free of the materialistic influences of the United States.

Rousseau, Jean-Jacques (1712-1778). French philosopher, social political theorist and writer of *The Social Contract.*

Rius Rivera, Juan (1846-1924). Fought for the liberation of Cuba and served as Civil Governor of Havana during the first years of the American occupation.

Ruiz Belvis, Segundo (1829-1867). Abolitionist and one of the writers of *Proyecto para la abolición de la esclavitud en Puerto Rico.*

Sanromá, Jesús María (1902-1984). Internationally famous pianist who distinguished himself by recording all the danzas composed by Juan Morel Campos.

Santos Chocanos, José (1867-1935). Peruvian poet and revolutionary who opposed American imperialism and advocated for the protection of indigenous people in Latin America.

Spengler, Oswald (1880-1936). German philosopher and writer of *The Decline of the West.*

Stahl, Agustín (1842-1917). Doctor who studied Puerto Rico's flora and fauna and shared his findings with the Natural History Museum of Germany, and other important scientific centers.

Tapia, Alejandro (1826-1882). Playwright, historian, novelist. *Mis memorias* is an autobiographical work. He also wrote *Biblioteca Histórica de Puerto Rico*, a collection of primary source documents on Puerto Rico dating back to the sixteenth century.

Tavárez, Manuel Gregorio (1843-1883). Father of the Puerto Rican danza, responsible for giving the musical genre a delicate and romantic touch making it suitable for concert salons.

Tomás Navarro, Tomás (1884-1979). Linguist and philologist who advocated teaching Spanish in Puerto Rico after the United States occupation.

Torres Vargas, Father Diego de (1590-1649). Commissioned by the Spanish crown to document the history of the island in the seventeenth century. It was called the *Description of the Island and City of Puerto Rico.*

Valero, Antonio de Bernabé (1790-1863). Military leader who believed in Puerto Rico's right to self-determination and in the federation of Latin American nations. He fought for the liberation of Cuba, and also with Simón Bolivar in Venezuela.

Valle, José del. Historian and sociologist. He wrote *Puerto Rico a Chicago: trabajos descriptivos y de investigaciones críticas.*

Varona, José Enrique (1849-1933). Writer, philosopher, poet and Vice President of the Republic of Cuba from 1913 to 1917.

Vizcarrondo, Julio (1830-1889). Abolitionist who helped found and fund Puerto Rico' s Ateneo, the island' s premiere repository of historical documents.

Zamacois, Eduardo (1876-1972). Spanish novelist born in Cuba who specialized in books embued with realism and eroticism.

Zeno Gandía, Manuel (1885-1930). One of Puerto Rico's outstanding novelists, he is known today primarily for the novel *La Charca,* first published in 1894.

Selected Bibliography

Alatas, Syed Hussein. *The Myth of the Lazy Native: A Study of the Image of the Malays, Filipinos, and Javanese from the Sixteenth to the Twentieth Century and Its Function in the Ideology of Colonial Capitalism.* Frank Cass, 1977.

Baldwin, James. *Notes of a Native Son.* Beacon Press, 1984.

---. *The Fire Next Time.* Vintage Books, 1993.

Barrell, John. *The Infection of Thomas de Quincey: A Psychopathology of Imperialism.* Yale University Press, 1991.

Bauer, Arnold J. *Goods, Power, History: Latin America's Material Culture (New Approaches to the Americas).* Cambridge University Press, 2001.

Briggs, Laura. *Reproducing Empire: Race, Sex, Science, and United States Imperialism in Puerto Rico.* University of California Press, 2002.

Cabán, Pedro A. *Constructing a Colonial People: Puerto Rico and the United States, 1898–1932.* Westview Press, 2000.

Davis, Darien J. *Avoiding the Dark: Race and the Forging of National Culture in Modern Brazil (Research in Migration and Ethnic Relations).* Ashgate Publishing Company, 1999.

Duany, Jorge. *The Puerto Rican Nation on the Move: Identities on the Island and in the United States.* University of North Carolina Press, 2002.

Selected Bibliography

Fanon, Frantz. *The Wretched of the Earth.* Grove Press, 1963.

Fernández Retamar, Roberto. *Caliban and Other Essays.* Translated by Edward Baker. University of Minnesota Press, 1989.

Fernández, Ronald. *The Disenchanted Island: Puerto Rico and the United States in the Twentieth Century.* Greenwood Publishing Group, 1992.

Flores, Juan. *Divided Borders: Essays on Puerto Rican Identity.* Arte Público Press, 1993.

González, José Luis. *Puerto Rico: The Four Storeyed Country and Other Essays.* Translated by Gerald Guinness. M. Weiner Publishers, 1993.

Hedrick, Tace. *Mestizo Modernism: Race, Nation and Identity in Latin American Culture, 1900–1940.* Rutgers University Press, 2003.

Kanellos, Nicolás, Dworkin y Méndez, Kenya, Balestra, Alejandra. *Herencia: The Anthology of Hispanic Literature of the United States (Recovering the United States Hispanic Literary Heritage).* Oxford University Press, 2001.

Maldonado Denis, Manuel. *Puerto Rico: A Socio-Historic Interpretation.* Vantage Press, 1972.

Marqués, René. *The Oxcart.* Translated by Charles Pilditch. Charles Scribner's Sons, 1969.

Montero, Oscar. *José Martí: An Introduction (New Directions in Latino American Culture).* Palgrave Macmillan, 2004.

Morris, Nancy. *Puerto Rico: Culture, Politics and Identity.* Praeger Publishers, 1995.

Naipaul, V. S. *A Bend in the River.* Vintage Books, 1989.

---. *East Indians in the Caribbean: Colonialism and the Struggle for Identity.* Kraus International Publications, 1981.

---. *India: A Wounded Civilization.* Vintage Books, 1977.

Negrón de Montilla, Aida. *Americanization in Puerto Rico and the Public School System.* Editorial Universitaria, 1975.

Pérez, Jr., Louis A. *On Becoming Cuban: Identity, Nationality, and Culture.* Ecco, 2001.

Phelps de Córdova, Loretta. *Five Centuries in Puerto Rico: Portraits and Eras.* Inter American University Press, 1988.

Said, Edward W. *Culture and Imperialism.* Random House, 1994.

Vasconcelos, José. *The Cosmic Race.* Translated by Didier T. Jaen. John Hopkins University Press, 1997.

Walcott, Derek. *What the Twilight Says: Essays.* Farrar, Straus and Giroux, 1998.

Williams, Eric E. *From Columbus to Castro: The History of the Caribbean, 1492–1969.* Harper & Row, 1971.

Index

Index